FOCUS ON THE FAMILY

Your Child

VIDEO SEMINAR

essentials of DISCIPLINE

What's OK, What's Not and What Works

with Dr. James Dobson
adapted by Steve and Anne Wamberg

Leader's Guide

TYNDALE

Tyndale House Publishers, Inc.
Wheaton, Illinois

Your Child Video Seminar: Essentials of Discipline, Leader's Guide

A Focus on the Family book published by Tyndale House Publishers, Wheaton, Illinois.

TYNDALE is a registered trademark of Tyndale House Publishers, Inc. Tyndale's quill logo is a trademark of Tyndale House Publishers, Inc.

Editors: John Duckworth & Mick Silva
Cover design: Peak Creative
Interior design: Angela Messinger
Interior illustration: Cornerstone Media

ISBN: 1-58997-190-6

Printed in the United States of America
1 2 3 4 5 6 7 8 9 / 10 09 08 07 06 05

TABLE OF CONTENTS

WELCOME!

Parenting can be tough—but learning about parenting doesn't have to be. In fact, we think you'll find this course easy to use, to the point—even fun.

At the heart of each session is a video presentation, adapted from the works of popular author, broadcaster, and psychologist Dr. James Dobson. Each video segment features animation that will capture your group's attention, down-to-earth advice from Dr. Dobson, and thought-provoking interviews with real-life parents.

Then there's the participant's guide—the book each of your group members will need to make the course personal. Parents read and complete portions of the book before each session. But this "homework" isn't a chore your group will dread, because the book is entertaining, interactive, and highly practical.

Finally, there's the leader's guide—the book you're holding right now. It's designed to help you turn the video and participant's guide into a lively group experience in which parents learn and support each other.

PREPARING FOR THE SESSION

Before each meeting, have group members read and complete these sections in the corresponding chapter of their participant's guides:
- "Home Base," a short, intriguing introduction from Dr. Dobson;
- "Your Story," an interactive way for parents to find out where they stand on the subject at hand; and
- "WordWorks," a brief Bible study.

You'll want to read and complete these sections yourself, too, as well as reviewing the session plan in the leader's guide. Preview the video segment, if possible; then make sure it's cued up for your group to watch, and that your player and monitor are ready.

For most sessions, you'll need pencils or pens. For some, you may need chalkboard or chalk or other display surface and writing tool (newsprint and marker, white board and marker, etc.). You may also need to gather a few other easy-to-find materials, listed in "Setting the Stage" at the start of each session.

LEADING THE SESSION

You'll find the session plan instructions in regular type; things you might say to the group are in bold type; suggested answers are in parentheses.

Each session, designed to last 45-60 minutes, includes five steps:

1. All in This Together (5-10 minutes)

Using a game or other "icebreaker" activity will help grab the group's interest and build a sense of community.

2. You Are Here (5-10 minutes)

Volunteers share responses they made to the "Your Story" section of the participant's guide.

3. Screen Time (15-30 minutes)

Watch and discuss the video segment. Group members can use the "Screen Time" section of the participant's guide for taking notes.

4. By the Book (5-10 minutes)

People talk about the answers they gave to the "WordWorks" Bible study section of the participant's guide.

5. Work It Out (10 minutes)

It's time for practical application, as group members use the "Your Way" section of the participant's guide to come up with action plans for their own families.

TIPS FOR SUCCESS

- If your group is like most, you often run out of time before you run out of discussion questions and activities. What to do? Simply choose the exercises and questions you think will be most meaningful to your group and concentrate on those. Try starting with the bare essentials—watching the video and applying the principles through the final "Work It Out" activity—and add steps as your schedule allows.
- Planning a 12-week course? Be sure to include an extra week for the review session at the end. This is a great opportunity for people to work further on nitty-gritty application to their unique households. On the other hand, if your group wants studies that last only a month, consider tackling only sessions 1-4, 5-8, or 9-12—and leaving the rest for another time.
- Invite discussion, but don't be surprised if some group members are reluctant to share personal information. It's hard to admit

one's mistakes as a parent—or to talk about painful childhood experiences. If people want to reflect silently on a probing question, encourage them to do so.

- It's a good idea to have a few extra copies of the participant's guide on hand, so that visitors (and those who forgot their books) can take part.
- If you don't have an answer to every parenting question, join the club! It's okay to say, "I don't know." Ask group members to share wisdom from their experience. Refer people to Dr. Dobson's books, especially *The Complete Marriage and Family Home Reference Guide* (Tyndale House). Encourage those who face especially difficult parenting situations to consult your pastor or a counselor.
- Have a good time! Parenting may be serious business, but most of your group members probably would appreciate a light touch as they learn. Let your group be a place where parents can enjoy each other and gain perspective on their child-rearing challenges.
- Pray. Pray for your group members during the week. Urge them to pray for each other. Ask God to help each person become the loving, effective parent he or she was meant to be.

Ready to have a lasting, positive impact on the lives of the families represented in your group? May God bless you as you lead!

SESSION 1

WHY YOUR CHILD NEEDS DISCIPLINE

SESSION AIM To help group members understand how parental authority benefits children, and how that authority can be shown through loving and consistent discipline.

SCRIPTURES FOR STUDY Deuteronomy 11:1-2; Psalm 94:12-13; Proverbs 1:1-7

SETTING THE STAGE
- Before the session, group members should read and complete these sections in chapter 1 of their participant's guides: "Home Base," "Your Story," and "WordWorks."
- Cue up the video to segment 1, "Why Your Child Needs Discipline."
- Prepare the cards for the "Don't Go There!" game as described in the "All in This Together" section of this session.
- You'll also need pencils or pens.

STARTING OUT Parents should not be surprised when rebellious or mischievous behavior occurs. It *will* happen, probably by the eighteenth month or before. Anyone who has watched a toddler throw a temper tantrum when she doesn't get her way must be hard pressed to explain how that expression of "innate goodness" got so mixed up! Did her mother or father model the tantrum for her, falling on the floor, slobbering, kicking, crying, and screaming? I would hope not. Either way, the kid needs no demonstration. Rebellion comes naturally to his and her entire generation—although in some individuals it is more pronounced than in others.

For this reason, parents can and must train, mold, correct, guide, punish, reward, instruct, warn, teach, and love their kids during the formative years. Their purpose is to shape that inner nature and keep it from tyrannizing the entire family. Ultimately, however, only Jesus Christ can cleanse it and make it "wholly acceptable" to the Master. This is what the Bible teaches about people, and this is what I firmly believe.

—Dr. James Dobson in *The Complete Marriage and Family Home Reference Guide* (Tyndale House)

STEP 1

ALL IN THIS TOGETHER

(5-10 minutes)

Ahead of the session, prepare for this activity by photocopying and cutting out the following cards (or make your own, using file cards and markers):

Begin the session with a game of "Don't Go There!" It's a fun way to break the ice and introduce the group to some terms you'll be using during this course.

Ask for five volunteers; give each a card. (If your group is large, you may want to form five teams and give a card to one person on each team.) The person with the card must not show it to anyone else. His or her job is to get the rest of the group (or team) to guess the word at the top of the card. He or she may use any word or phrase as a clue—*except* the "Don't Go There!" words listed under the word to be guessed.

For example, the player holding the "authority" card might give this clue: "person in charge." The group might guess, "boss." Once a "Don't Go There!" word has been said by the group, the cardholder is free to "go there" and use that word as a clue.

There's no winner or loser in this game. Just have fun laughing and being exposed to words you'll all be throwing around frequently in this course.

AUTHORITY

BOSS
LEADER
OFFICIAL
POWER
EXPERT

DISCIPLINE

RESTRAINT
SELF-CONTROL
PUNISHMENT
CORRECTION
REGULATION

SPANK

SWAT
BOTTOM
PADDLE
SMACK

CORPORAL
PUNISHMENT

ANGER

TEMPER
RAGE
IRRITATION
ANNOYANCE
BOILING POINT

REWARD

BRIBE
INCENTIVE
COMPLIMENT
RECOGNITION
PRIZE

When you're done with the game, make a connection to this session's topic by asking questions like these:

When it comes to disciplining kids, is there any topic about which you'd like to say, "Don't go there!"? Why?

Are there any aspects of discipline you hope we _do_ address? Why?

STEP 2

YOU ARE HERE

(5-10 minutes)

Ask group members to turn to the "Your Story" section in the participant's guide. Invite them to share some of their responses from this section as they feel comfortable. Many of the questions are light-hearted and probably will generate amusing responses. Still, remember that some answers may be quite personal, so group members might not want to share everything.

During this discussion and throughout the course, try to be especially sensitive to any who recall difficult childhoods during which discipline was administered harshly or not at all. Some parents may also express frustration about their current efforts to keep their kids "in line." If needed, offer to talk later with any group members who reveal serious problems—or privately refer them to your pastor or a counselor.

After giving volunteers a chance to tell "where they are" on these issues, thank them for their honesty. You may want to wrap up this part of the discussion with comments like these:

Some of us don't have fond memories of how we were disciplined as children. Some of us may not be too proud of the way we're handling discipline now. But this isn't a group for "perfect" parents. We're here to learn together about how to have the "happy endings" we want for our kids—no matter what mistakes we or our parents may have made in the past.

STEP 3

SCREEN TIME

(15-30 minutes)

Before viewing video segment 1, you may want to introduce Dr. James Dobson, who is featured in this series. Feel free to adapt this biographical "blurb" for your group:

Dr. James Dobson is the founder and president of Focus on the Family, an organization dedicated to the preservation of the home.

His radio broadcast is heard on stations around the world, and his commentaries air on television as well.

A licensed psychologist, Dr. Dobson holds a Ph.D. in child development from the University of Southern California. He served on the faculty of the University of Southern California School of Medicine for 14 years and on the attending staff of Children's Hospital of Los Angeles for 17 years. He has also been a public school teacher and counselor.

The author of several best-selling books on parenting and marriage, Dr. Dobson has advised U.S. presidents on family issues—and been appointed to several government commissions. Perhaps most importantly, he's the father of two grown children, Danae and Ryan, and the husband of Shirley.

Pass out pencils or pens. Watch video segment 1, entitled, "Why Your Child Needs Discipline." Encourage group members to use the "Screen Time" section of the participant's guide for taking notes.

After viewing the video segment, discuss it—using questions and comments like the following.

Which of these words best describes your feelings about what you just saw: reassuring, threatening, challenging, freeing, or restricting? Why?

In the video, "expert" Dr. O'Blivious wanted to let children raise themselves. Can you think of any problems that come up when kids are left on their own to determine their boundaries? (Examples: They do dangerous things because they don't understand the risks; they think parents don't care enough to set limits; they learn to see themselves as the final authorities on everything.)

Do you know any parents that follow Dr. O'Blivious' school of thought? Why do you think they place such a high premium on freedom from restraints? (Allow volunteers to respond as time allows.)

Did you agree with the sentiment raised by the mother interviewed who didn't like being the bad guy? What was Dr. Dobson's advice? (Discipline is not something you do to a child; it's something that's done for him or her because kids need to know where the boundaries are.)

Do you think most parents today are too strict or too permissive? Why?

Before seeing this video, had you thought much about your goals in raising kids? What would you say has been your main objective so far?

What were the two parenting objectives Dr. Dobson mentioned

that need to be balanced? (First, helping our kids to understand that we love them; second, teaching our kids control and to respect our leadership as parents.)

According to Dr. Dobson, it is a primary objective of parenting to keep the two essential ingredients, love and control, in proper balance.

Are you comfortable with that definition? Why or why not?

How does setting boundaries or limits help a child feel more secure? (The child knows what the rules are, who's available to enforce them, and that he's safe within those boundaries.)

Would anyone be willing to share an example of something you feel needs correction in your child? (Allow as many responses as time allows.)

STEP 4

BY THE BOOK

(5-10 minutes)

Have group members turn to the chapter 1 "WordWorks" Bible study section of the participant's guide. Encourage volunteers to call out answers to the questions found there.

1. PSALM 94:12-13

Do you think of discipline as a "blessing"? Why or why not? (Answers will vary. Some may say discipline is a blessing because it keeps one from developing a pattern of trouble, or shows how to please God. Others, especially those who recall being punished unfairly, may express doubts.)

Do your kids think of discipline as a good thing? Have you ever tried to get them to see it that way? If so, what happened?

How could discipline grant someone "relief from days of trouble"? Has that ever happened for you? (By providing boundaries and consequences, discipline can prevent future bad choices and actions. Participants can offer their own examples.)

How could discipline spare your child(ren) trouble in the future? (Discipline helps develop security, self-confidence, and self-discipline, which make it easier for kids to make good choices; it also reinforces positive values and discourages uncivil or antisocial behavior.)

2. PROVERBS 1:1-7

Discipline is tied to a whole shopping list of favorable character traits in this passage. Which three would you most like to see in your child(ren)?

This passage says that "the fear [an awed respect] of the LORD is the beginning of knowledge." If a child doesn't have this respect for God, how does it make the job of disciplining harder for a parent? Do you feel your children have this foundation? How can you tell? (A lack of respect for God makes it unlikely that a child would respect the authority God has delegated to others, including parents. That means a child could treat a parent's correction lightly, or ignore it altogether. Children demonstrate respect for God by acknowledging Him—for example, through prayer, in conversation, or in worship.)

Take a look at that "shopping list" again. Do you see your child(ren) making progress in any of those areas? If so, how might your discipline have helped? (Encourage group members to share successes, even small ones.)

3. DEUTERONOMY 11:1-2

When you read about "the discipline of the Lord," what feelings and images come to your mind? (Responses will depend upon participants' experiences with God. Some might talk about a guiding hand, a twinge of conscience, or a sense of being corrected by the Holy Spirit. Others might think of judgment, lightning strikes, a personal disaster, feelings of guilt, or being taken to the proverbial woodshed.)

What would you like your child(ren) to feel and think when they hear a phrase like "the discipline of the Lord"? (Some possibilities: A loving hand that leads us back to the right path; feelings of security, warmth, correction with love.)

What do you think your role should be in telling your child(ren) about God's discipline? (Answers will vary. Rather than offering a "right" answer, encourage group members to keep thinking about how they might discuss this side of God's nature with their kids.)

STEP 5

WORK IT OUT

(10 minutes)

Have the group turn to the "Your Way" section in chapter 1 of the participant's guide. Give people at least five minutes to work through the activities individually. If time is short, have each person choose one or two questions to address and leave the rest to work on at home.

During the last few minutes, form pairs. Encourage partners to tell each other one "action step" they plan to take this week in response to what they've learned. If time allows, and if group members are comfortable doing so, ask partners to pray for each other as they plan to take action.

In closing, urge group members to find further advice at home in this session's "Tech Support" section of the participant's guide. Encourage them also to read and complete the "Home Base," "Your Story," and "WordWorks" sections in chaper 2 before your next meeting.

SESSION 2

IRRESPONSIBILITY vs. DEFIANCE

SESSION AIM | To help group members tell the difference between childish irresponsibility and willful defiance, and to help them discipline lovingly and effectively in cases of the latter.

SCRIPTURES FOR STUDY | Proverbs 5:11-14, 22-23; 13:18; 15:5; 19:18; 22:15; Hebrews 12:11

SETTING THE STAGE | • Before the session, group members should read and complete these sections in chapter 2 of their participant's guides: "Home Base," "Your Story," and "WordWorks."
• Cue up the video to segment 2, "When Should You Discipline?"
• You'll also need pencils or pens, plus chalkboard and chalk (or other display surface and writing tool).

STARTING OUT | When mothers and fathers fail to take charge in moments of challenge, they create for themselves and their families a potential lifetime of heartache. That's what happened in the case of the Holloways, who were parents of a teen named Becky (not their real names). Mr. Holloway came to see me in desperation one afternoon and related the cause for his concern. Becky had never been required to obey or respect her parents, and her early years were a strain on the entire family. Mrs. Holloway was confident Becky would eventually become more manageable, but that never happened. She held her parents in utter contempt from her youngest childhood and was sullen, disrespectful, selfish, and uncooperative. Mr. and Mrs. Holloway did not feel they had the right to make demands on their daughter, so they smiled politely and pretended not to notice her horrid behavior.

Their magnanimous attitude became more difficult to maintain as Becky steamrolled into puberty and adolescence. . . . They thought a party might make her happy, and Mrs. Holloway worked very hard to decorate the house and prepare refreshments. On the appointed evening, a mob of dirty, profane teens swarmed into the house, breaking and destroying the furnishings. During the course of the evening, Mrs. Holloway said something that angered Becky. The girl struck her mother and left her lying in a pool of blood in the bathroom. . . .

Parents like the Holloways often fail to understand how love and discipline interact to influence the attitudes of a child. These two aspects of a relationship are not opposites working against each other. . . . That simple understanding when Becky was younger could have spared the Holloways an adolescent nightmare.

Their attitude when Becky rebelled as a preschooler should have been, "I love you too much to let you behave like that."

—Dr. James Dobson in *The New Dare to Discipline* (Tyndale House)

STEP 1

ALL IN THIS TOGETHER

(5-10 minutes)

Try starting the meeting with a fun activity that builds a sense of community among your group members. You might call it, "Where Do You Draw the Line?"

Begin by asking people to call out examples of limits that parents typically must place on a child's behavior. These might include bedtimes, frequency of bathing, curfew deadlines, TV shows that may be watched, etc. Write these on a chalkboard or other display surface.

Now choose one of the limit categories ("Names You May Call Your Sister," for example). Ask group members to suggest ten items to list in this category, from most acceptable to least acceptable. (If the category is name-calling, items might range from "Sis" to "Speedy" to "Doofus" to "Stinking Humongous Toad.") Write these items in a vertical column.

Next, ask a volunteer to come up and draw a line between two of the items on the list to show where he or she would "draw the line" between acceptable and unacceptable behavior. Have one or two other volunteers do the same; see whether everyone draws the line in the same place.

Then ask: **Once you've drawn the line, what do you do if your child crosses it?**

Let group members respond. Don't worry if there's disagreement over where to draw the lines or how to respond when the line is crossed. If time allows, have fun doing the same with one or two more of the categories participants created.

Then introduce the session topic with comments like these:

Knowing where—and when—to draw the line is a crucial part of parenting. Knowing what to do when the line is crossed can affect our kids for the rest of their lives. That's what this session is about.

STEP 2

YOU ARE HERE

(5-10 minutes)

Call group members' attention to the "Your Story" section in the participant's guide. Invite them to share a few of their responses to the survey; avoid pressing for information, however, since answers in this section may be quite personal.

Many of the items on the survey address feelings and opinions, so looking for "right" answers isn't necessary. As needed, however, you may want to supplement group members' comments on certain parts of the survey with the following observations.

Item 2: You should start disciplining children when they're 18 months old.

Dr. Dobson's friend, Nashville pediatrician Dr. Bill Slonecker, once said, "If discipline begins on the second day of life, you're one day late." He didn't mean that babies should be spanked; they shouldn't. Even shaking a child before the age of 18 months can cause brain damage. Dr. Slonecker was talking about the need to lead children, even at the earliest age. The decision of whether to take an infant's temperature, for instance, must be the parent's—not the child's.

Item 4: Children should be punished for making a mess.

As explained in this session's video segment, accidents don't warrant punishment. But if the mess is deliberate, or if a child refuses to clean it up and is capable of doing so, disciplinary action is in order.

Item 6: It's usually best to ignore it when kids misbehave.

If it's childish irresponsibility, that may be appropriate. But if it's disobedience, the challenge should be met. Dr. Dobson helps parents distinguish between these behaviors in this session's video.

Item 7: Teenagers are too old to be disciplined.

Discipline takes different forms during adolescence, but it's still important. See the "Tech Support" section of the participant's guide for an amusing and enlightening story about Dr. Dobson's experience with this during his own teenage years.

Item 10: Requiring your children to obey will hurt them in the long run.

The word "requiring" may remind some of jackboots and whips; discipline should never be cruel or loveless. But the fact is that *not* holding children responsible for "crossing the line" is much more likely to hurt them later. Parents need to draw their lines wisely, though, not arbitrarily.

If group members are willing, have a few of them explain the "line in the sand" incidents they described or drew at the end of the "Your Story" section. What did they learn from those experiences?

STEP 3

SCREEN TIME

(15-30 minutes)

Pass out pencils or pens. Watch video segment 2, entitled, "Irresponsibility vs. Defiance." Encourage group members to use the "Screen Time" section of the participant's guide for taking notes.

After viewing the video segment, discuss it—using questions and comments like the following.

Remember the first Mini-Maxi Mart cartoon? Could you relate to that?

What did you think that mom should have done?

What would you have done? Why?

Speaking of battles in supermarkets and other public places, Dr. Dobson has some helpful things to say on the subject. Share the following quote from Dr. Dobson's book *The Complete Marriage and Family Home Reference Guide* (Tyndale House):

"If [children] are going to pick a fight with Mom or Dad, they'd rather stage it in a public place, such as a supermarket or in the church foyer. They are smart enough to know that they are 'safer' in front of other people. They will grab candy or speak in disrespectful ways that would never be attempted at home. . . .

"You may be one of the parents who has fallen into the trap of creating 'sanctuaries' in which the old rules aren't enforced. . . . I recommend that you lay out the ground rules before you enter those public arenas, making it clear that the same rules will apply. Then if he misbehaves, simply take him back to the car or around the corner and do what you would have done at home. His public behavior will improve dramatically."

Give participants a few moments to react to this advice if they wish. Then move on:

Of course, not every instance of misbehavior is about testing limits. In the video Dr. Dobson talks about something called childish irresponsibility. What is that? (Accidents like forgetting things, losing things, spilling things.)

How is that different from willful defiance? (Willful defiance is intentional; it's a refusal to accept parental leadership.)

Dr. Dobson talked about a game kids play—"Challenge the Chief." Why is it important to meet that challenge? (It's a test of parental leadership; children want and need to be led, but insist that parents earn the right to lead them by standing up to these challenges; ignoring the challenges could encourage rebellion.)

Dr. Dobson says that when our kids challenge us, they're asking a question. What is it? ("Are you though enough to make me do what you say?")

So when should we discipline? (When parental authority is challenged by willful defiance.)

What are the principles of earning the right to lead? (Define the boundaries in advance, respond with confident decisiveness, distinguish defiance from irresponsibility, reassure and teach afterwards, avoid impossible demands, let love guide.)

If we don't need to punish kids when they're simply acting their age, does that mean childish irresponsibility shouldn't have consequences? What if your toddler accidentally breaks your antique glassware—or your teenager absent-mindedly locks the keys in the car for the twelfth time? Should you just ignore it?

Let group members react. If time allows, ask them to suggest appropriate responses that could help a child avoid careless or forgetful behavior. (Examples: keeping breakable items away from a toddler; making a particular room off limits; letting a teen who locks the keys in the car walk home.)

STEP 4

BY THE BOOK

(5-10 minutes)

Next, have the group turn to "WordWorks," the Bible study section of the participant's guide. Let volunteers call out answers to the questions found there.

1. PROVERBS 5:11-14
What three words might describe the feelings of this person who's looking back on his or her life? (Some possibilities: regretful, sorry, embarrassed.)

What does that tell you about the value of discipline? (It has a long-term impact; the lack of it can ruin a person's life.)

2. PROVERBS 5:22-23; 13:18; 19:18
According to these verses, what can eventually happen to a child who hasn't been disciplined? What kinds of "death" could a lack of discipline lead to? (Poverty, shame, and literal death. "Death" might mean physical destruction due to recklessness or spiritual death due to a rejection of the truth.)

3. PROVERBS 15:5
Children have a choice of whether to spurn or heed discipline. How can a parent show that it's better to heed than to spurn? (By rewarding kids for obeying and penalizing them for defiance.)

4. PROVERBS 22:15
How does this verse contrast with the view that children are a "blank slate" at birth, and that they'll do the right thing unless parents teach them otherwise? (These passages imply that our natural tendency, even as children, is often to do the wrong thing.)

What will happen if a parent doesn't deal with a child's challenges to his or her authority? (A child who's left to be his or her own authority is likely to be headed for trouble.)

5. HEBREWS 12:11
How could this verse help a parent with the stress of having to confront a defiant child? (By helping him or her see that confrontation is worth it over the long term, and ultimately benefits the child.)

STEP 5

WORK IT OUT

(10 minutes)

Have the group turn to the "Your Way" section in the participant's guide. After passing out pencils or pens, give people at least five minutes to work through the activities individually.

Then form pairs or small groups. In the time that remains, let volunteers share with their partners what they learned or planned. Make it clear, though, that no one needs to feel pressured to reveal answers.

Before closing, share the following caution from Dr. Dobson on discerning the causes of seemingly defiant behavior—quoted from *The New Dare to Discipline* (Tyndale House):

"I must point out that some rebellious behavior is distinctly different in origin from the 'challenging' defiance I've been describing. A child's antagonism and stiff-lipped negativism may emanate from frustration, disappointment, or rejection, and must be interpreted as a warning signal to be heeded. Perhaps the toughest task in parenthood is recognizing the difference between these two distinct motives. . . .

"The most effective parents are those who have the skill to get behind the eyes of their child, seeing what he sees, thinking what he thinks, feeling what he feels. For example, when a two-year-old screams and cries at bedtime, one must ascertain what he is communicating. If he is genuinely frightened by the blackness of his room, the appropriate response should be quite different than if he is merely protesting about having to go nighty-night. The art of good parenthood revolves around the interpretation of meaning behind behavior."

Close by having partners pray about the requests they wrote at the end of the "Your Story" section. Encourage all to read the "Tech Support" tips from Dr. Dobson in the participant's guide as they seek this week to carry out what they've learned—and to read and complete the "Home Base," "Your Story," and "WordWorks" sections before your next meeting.

Session 3

Anger vs. Action

Session Aim To help group members evaluate whether they tend to rely on anger or action in disciplining their children, and to show them why and how to take action instead of merely getting mad.

Scriptures for Study Psalm 6:1; Proverbs 15:1; James 1:19, 20; Revelation 3:19

Setting the Stage
- Before the session, group members should read and complete these sections in chapter 3 of their participant's guides: "Home Base," "Your Story," and "WordWorks."
- Cue up the video to segment 3, "Anger and Action."
- You'll also need pencils or pens, plus copies of the role plays found in "All in This Together" (step 1).

Starting Out Yelling and nagging at children can become a habit, and an ineffectual one at that! Have you ever screamed at your child, "This is the last time I'm telling you for the last time!"? Parents often use anger to get action instead of using action to get action. It is exhausting and it doesn't work! Trying to control children by screaming is as utterly futile as trying to steer a car by honking the horn. . . .

When a youngster discovers there is no threat behind the millions of words he hears, he stops listening to them. The only messages he responds to are those reaching a peak of emotion, which means there is much screaming and yelling going on. The child is pulling in the opposite direction, fraying Mom's nerves and straining the parent-child relationship. But the most important limitation of those verbal reprimands is that their user often has to resort to physical punishment in the end anyway. It is also more likely to be severe, because the adult is irritated and out of control. Thus, instead of the discipline being administered in a calm and judicious manner, the parent has become unnerved and frustrated, swinging wildly at the belligerent child. There was no reason for a fight to have occurred. The situation could have ended very differently if the parental attitude had been one of confident serenity.

—Dr. James Dobson in *The New Dare to Discipline* (Tyndale House)

STEP 1

ALL IN THIS TOGETHER

(5-10 minutes)

Start this session by getting dramatic—with some role plays.

Form four teams. Give the first two teams copies of Role Play 1, which follows. Team 1 should act out how to resolve the conflict with anger; Team 2 should resolve it without anger.

Give the other two teams copies of Role Play 2, which also follows. Team 3 should act out how to resolve the conflict with anger; Team 4 should resolve it without anger. (Note: If your group is too small to field four teams, form just two and give them only one of the role plays.)

Role Play 1: You've been on a long trip with your family. You're on the way home, but still have more than a day's drive ahead of you. Your kids (and their parents!) are tired and cranky. As the day wears on, the kids pick at each other more and more. Nothing you say, not even your threats, seems to make any difference in their behavior. How can you resolve this?

> **Role Play 2:** More times than you can remember, you've asked your kids to pick up after themselves. Now there are dirty socks in the hall, CDs lying all over the living room, school books and papers scattered "from here to tomorrow." Your kids say they'll pick it up, but never seem to get around to it. You're tired of being the one to finally get it done, quick, before someone comes over! How do you resolve this?

Let the groups plan their presentations for a couple of minutes. Then have each present its role play in front of the others.

After the presentations, discuss—using questions like the following:

Which resolution do you think would happen in real life? Why?

Which resolution do you think would be most effective? Why?

Tell which resolution you think kids would respond to better, and why.

Which resolution do you think is better for the parents? Why?

Introduce the topic for this session with comments like these:

Everybody gets angry! And a lot of us assume anger is a necessary part of discipline, even though it wears us out. But is it? And does it work? Let's find out in this session.

STEP 2

YOU ARE HERE

(5-10 minutes)

During this step, have group members stay in the teams you formed for the role plays.

Ask people to turn to the "Your Story" section in chapter 3 of the participant's guide. Invite them to share some of their responses from this section with other team members. Some group members may not want to say much, being reluctant to admit that they get mad at their children. Assure the group that all parents get angry sometimes. Affirm, too, that no one has to reveal personal information that would make him or her uncomfortable.

You may want to invite anyone who feels his or her anger is out of control at home to talk later with you or your pastor.

After giving people a chance to tell "where they are" on these issues, thank them for their honesty. You may want to wrap up this part of the discussion with comments like these:

The purpose of this session isn't to make us feel guilty about getting angry. It's to examine how we use anger when we discipline—and how to avoid what Dr. James Dobson calls "the biggest mistake parents make."

STEP 3

SCREEN TIME

(15-30 minutes)

Pass out pencils or pens. Watch video segment 3, entitled, "Anger and Action." Encourage group members to use the "Screen Time" section of the participant's guide for taking notes.

After viewing the video segment, discuss it. Use questions and comments like these:

Have you ever felt like the mom in the cartoon? When?

Why do so many parents rely on anger to keep their kids under control? (Answers may vary. Some parents may simply be imitating their own parents' example. But the main reason probably is that many parents don't take action until their anger boils over, if ever—and mistakenly conclude that the anger "worked.")

Do you agree with the idea that anger alone doesn't change children's behavior? Why or why not? (Many will probably agree, having recognized their own pattern of loud and angry-sounding threats that have had little effect.)

What is the point beyond which your kids know they can't push you without getting disciplined?

How would your children respond if they knew that you'd put discipline into action immediately after you spoke the first time?

Participants may mention how surprised their children would be. Some may note that there would be initial conflict in instituting an "I speak once and expect you to obey" policy. Others may realize that there would be long-term benefits, starting with the reduction of the tension level at home.

What are some of the most effective actions you've taken when disciplining your kids?

According to the video, it doesn't take much action to avoid conflict if what? (If the child is convinced that you mean it, and you're willing to implement it.)

What would be hardest for you about following the advice in this video?

What might be the greatest benefit to you as a parent? To your child?

Accept as many responses as time allows, then say, **As Dr. Dobson said, the ultimate benefit of removing anger from the confrontation is the freedom to discipline in love.**

STEP 4

BY THE BOOK

(5-10 minutes)

Ask the participants to turn to "WordWorks," the Bible study section of the participant's guide. Let volunteers call out their answers to the questions found there.

1. PSALM 6:1

In this verse, David—a man known for his close relationship with God—prays that God wouldn't discipline him in anger. Why do you suppose he prayed that way? (David probably was asking for mercy, knowing that God's power could easily destroy anyone who was the object of His anger. David may have been considering how the anger of humans, who are far less powerful, had caused damage.)

Did your parents ever discipline you in anger? Did the anger help or hurt? Answers will vary. Some participants may have deeply personal reasons for their responses; avoid pressing for replies, staying sensitive to how much people are willing to share.

2. JAMES 1:19, 20

Can a parent who follows this advice be effective in disciplining his or her children? Why or why not?

As needed, observe that listening to a child lets the child know you're considering his or her side of the story before you discipline. Taking your time before saying anything allows you to choose words carefully. Being slow to anger might help you discipline calmly and rationally, without overreacting; it could also give you time to take level-headed action before emotions take over.

This verse implies that our anger doesn't accomplish God's purposes. In your experience, does being angry at your kids help to "keep them in line"? Why or why not?

Answers will vary, but participants may realize that being angry at their children has little positive impact—while action without anger gets results.

Why might it be wise to keep your anger under control as you discipline a child? (Some possibilities: to stay in control of your thoughts and actions; to avoid child abuse; to keep your blood pressure down.)

3. PROVERBS 15:1

Do you think your child(ren) would describe your discipline as gentle or harsh? How would you describe it? Answers will vary; some group members may not want to reply at all if you've "hit a nerve." If you don't get much response, encourage people to think about the question this week.

What role does anger usually play in your approach to discipline? Are you satisfied with that? Again, be sensitive to how much participants want to reveal about themselves. It's likely, however, that at least some of your group members want to improve the way they handle anger and discipline.

4. REVELATION 3:19

Jesus is speaking in this verse. How would you describe His motivation for discipline? (Love.)

What seems to be His goal? (To get us to turn from wrongdoing—to repent.)

To "repent" means to be sincerely sorry and to change your behavior accordingly. Does adding anger to discipline make it more likely that a child will repent, or less likely? Why?

As needed, point out that many children tend to respond defensively to anger—putting on a "tough guy" act, becoming stoic, talking back, or otherwise rebelling—rather than seeing their need to change.

STEP 5

WORK IT OUT

(10 minutes)

Have the group turn to the "Your Way" section in the participant's guide. Allow at least five minutes to work through the activities individually.

Re-form the teams you used earlier. Let volunteers tell each other what they've learned, or what goals they've set for the coming days. Assure the group that no one is required to disclose his or her answers.

Your discussion about parental anger may generate guilt feelings in some of your group members. Before you close the session, read the following encouragement from Dr. Dobson, quoted from *The Complete Marriage and Family Home Reference Guide* (Tyndale House):

"I doubt if it is too late to do things right, although your ability to influence your children lessens with the passage of time. Fortunately we are permitted to make many mistakes with our kids. They are resilient, and they usually survive most of our errors in judgment. It's a good thing they do, because none of us can be a perfect parent. Besides, it's not the occasional mistakes that hurt a child—it is the consistent influence of destructive conditions throughout childhood that does the damage."

Encourage participants to give themselves room to change and grow as parents. Then close the session by having teams pray together about the goals people have set for the week ahead.

Remind group members to read the "Tech Support" tips in the participant's guide to help them stay on track in meeting their goals—and to read and complete the "Home Base," "Your Story," and "WordWorks" sections before your next meeting.

SESSION 4

FINDING BALANCE IN DISCIPLINE

SESSION AIM   To help group members understand how to balance love and control as they discipline their children.

SCRIPTURES FOR STUDY   Jeremiah 31:18-20; Hebrews 12:4-10

SETTING THE STAGE
- Before the session, group members should read and complete these sections in chapter 4 of their participant's guides: "Home Base," "Your Story," and "WordWorks."
- Cue up the video to segment 4, "Disciplining with Love."
- You'll also need pencils or pens, plus milk chocolate, baker's chocolate, and a serving plate (see step 1).

STARTING OUT   The principles of good parenting are eternal, having originated with the Creator of families. The inspired concepts in Scripture have been handed down generation after generation and are just as valid for the twenty-first century as they were for our ancestors. Unfortunately, many of today's parents have never heard those time-honored ideas and have no clue about what they're trying to accomplish at home. . . .

Much has been written about the dangers of harsh, oppressive, unloving discipline; these warnings are valid and should be heeded. However, the consequences of oppressive discipline have been cited as justification for the abdication of leadership. That is foolish. There are times when a strong-willed child will clench his little fists and dare his parents to accept his challenges. He is not motivated by frustration or inner hostility, as it is often supposed. He merely wants to know where the boundaries lie and who's available to enforce them.

Many well-meaning specialists have waved the banner of tolerance, but offered no solution for defiance. They have stressed the importance of parental understanding of the child, and I concur. But we need to teach children that they have a few things to learn about their parents, too!

—Dr. James Dobson in *The New Dare to Discipline* (Tyndale House)

STEP 1

ALL IN THIS TOGETHER

(5-10 minutes)

Before the session, buy two kinds of chocolate—milk chocolate and baker's chocolate. Both come in bar form, and both are brown—but there the similarity ends. Milk chocolate is sweet, while baker's chocolate is completely unsweetened and guaranteed to bring a grimace to the face of anyone who eats it.

Break the chocolate into pieces and put it on a serving plate. Mix the pieces up.

Start the session by offering chocolate to members of the group. Those who get milk chocolate will most likely enjoy it, while those who get the other kind may run to the nearest trash can.

Give the unfortunates who got baker's chocolate a chance to have some milk chocolate. Then explain what happened. Ask: **What's the difference between these two kinds of chocolate?** (Sweetener.)

Even a small amount of sweetener can make a huge difference. A well-known child expert—I believe it was Mary Poppins—once said, "A spoonful of sugar helps the medicine go down."

In a way, sugar does for medicine what love does for discipline.

Discipline without love is a harsh and bitter experience. In this session we'll discover how to make sure we don't miss that vital ingredient of love.

STEP 2

YOU ARE HERE

(5-10 minutes)

Call attention to the "Your Story" section in the participant's guide. Ask (but don't press) group members to explain how they completed the exercises there.

As needed, you may want to supplement people's answers with information like the following.

Item 1: If you had to choose, would you rather be called a "permissive" parent or an "authoritarian" parent?

Group members may get bogged down in trying to define the words "permissive" and "authoritarian." If so, explain that for purposes of this discussion, "permissive" means "overly lenient," while "authoritarian" means "requiring absolute obedience at the expense of individual freedom."

Do you think you tend to be more permissive or authoritarian? Why? On the following scale, circle a number to show how comfortable you are with your answer to the previous question.

Some group members may not want to reveal this personal information, but encourage those who do to explain misgivings they might have about their disciplinary styles. Do they simply dislike the labels of "permissive" and "authoritarian"? Do they fear that their kids are out of control or too tightly controlled and likely to rebel later?

Item 2: Finish this sentence: If love is like a balloon, control is like . . .

Ask volunteers to explain their responses. Encourage participants to keep an open mind to the idea that love and control are both positive concepts, as will be noted in this session's video segment.

Item 3: When it comes to discipline, how well do you balance love and control? Draw yourself on the seesaw below to show your answer.

If some group members aren't sure what it means to balance love and control, explain that you'll all learn more about that in this session's video.

Now put an X on the seesaw to show where you think your child(ren) would draw you. Is there a difference? If so, why?

If group members are willing to share their answers to these questions, encourage them to explain why their perceptions may differ from those of their children. Are such differences inevitable, or can parents learn something from them?

STEP 3

SCREEN TIME

(15-30 minutes)

Pass out pencils or pens. Watch video segment 4, entitled, "Disciplining with Love." Encourage group members to use the "Screen Time" section of the participant's guide for taking notes.

After viewing the video segment, discuss it together, using questions and comments like the following:

What would Goldilocks find if she came to your house? Did you see yourself in any of the bear families?

Can you be "too loving" when it comes to discipline?

That may depend on one's definition of "loving." If parents equate love with not setting limits for a child, they can fall into permissiveness (fearing that limits will make the child feel unloved) or authoritarianism (fearing "love" will spoil the child). But setting appropriate limits and enforcing them with appropriate discipline are expressions of love—and should be done in a way that helps the child to see them as loving acts.

How can you help a child understand that you discipline because you love him or her?

Let the group offer suggestions. If you like, use the following quote from Dr. Dobson's book, *The New Dare to Discipline*, as an example:

"'I love you too much to let you behave like that.' For the small child, word pictures can help convey this message more clearly. The following is a story I used with our very young children when they crossed the line of unacceptable behavior:

"'I knew of a little bird who was in his nest with his mommy. The mommy bird went off to find some worms to eat, and she told the little bird not to get out of the nest while she was gone. But the little bird didn't mind her. He jumped out of the nest and fell to the ground where a big cat got him. When I tell you to mind me, it is because I know what is best for you, just as the mommy bird did with her baby bird. When I tell you to stay in the front yard, it's because I don't want you to run in the street and get hit by a car. I love you, and I don't want anything to happen to you. If you don't mind me, I'll have to spank you to help you remember how important it is. Do you understand?'"

Dr. Dobson recommended parents work to understand the needs of their children. What were some of the needs he mentioned? (When he's lonely, he needs your company; when he's defiant, he needs your help in controlling his impulses; when he's afraid, he needs the security of your embrace; when he's happy, he needs to share his laughter and joy with those he loves.)

STEP 4

BY THE BOOK

(5-10 minutes)

Have group members turn to the "WordWorks" Bible study section of the participant's guide. Discuss their answers, using comments like the following.

1. JEREMIAH 31:18-20

These verses describe the way God disciplined Ephraim, a people of the nation of Judah. How would you describe the relationship between God and Ephraim? How did God seem to feel about His people? (The relationship between God and Ephraim seems to be one of honesty and closeness; Ephraim is willing to own up to the need for discipline and to change behavior to make the relationship close again. It's clear that God still loves Ephraim and wants Ephraim to know and accept it.)

By the time this dialogue between Ephraim and God took place, what had Ephraim realized about discipline? (There are many ways to say this, but Ephraim recognized that God's discipline was completely right. Discipline was the means to catch Ephraim's attention and led to some necessary changes.)

Does God seem more interested here in controlling His people or loving them? How are the two concepts connected? What kind of balance does He strike? (Responses may vary, though chances are that many group members will recognize that God is interested in both love and control. God's love for Ephraim led Him to want the best for Ephraim; the latter's disobedience put Ephraim in danger; until Ephraim figured things out, God exercised a degree of control through discipline.)

How does God's approach to discipline here compare with your own? (Answers will vary; some parents may mention their lack of perfection in comparison with God. As needed, point out that we should follow God's example of controlling our children when it's necessary for their good—because we love them, and in a loving way.)

2. HEBREWS 12:4-10

Does God's approach to discipline here sound loving to you? Why or why not?

People's reactions, should they choose to share them, may depend on their own experiences with their earthly fathers. If some group members struggle with this question, avoid trying to "correct" them. As needed, acknowledge that some may think this Scripture suggests that God disciplines just to make sure His children undergo punishment at some time. But the heart of the passage is that God's intent in discipline is to produce positive changes in us.

If your parents didn't discipline you, what might you conclude about their feelings toward you? (Some children might like the idea at first, but in the long run most probably would question whether their parents cared about them or their actions.)

Someone has said that the opposite of love isn't hate—it's indifference. How does this passage reflect that idea? (Discipline shows that God cares for us as His children. Discipline is a sign of relationship; applied with love, it's a sign of concern about a child's future.)

Do you think your children see your discipline as an expression of your love? Why or why not?

Answers will vary. Let group members respond according to their comfort level.

STEP 5

WORK IT OUT

(10 minutes)

Have the group turn to the "Your Way" section in the participant's guide. Allow at least five minutes for people to work through the activities individually. If time is short, have each person choose one or two questions to address and leave the rest to work on at home.

Wrap up the session with the following quote from Dr. Dobson's *The Complete Marriage and Family Home Reference Guide* (Tyndale House):

"The parent must be convinced that loving discipline is not something he or she does *to* the child; it is something done *for* the child."

Close this session by praying together. Ask God to prepare the hearts of the children who will be receiving the poems written in the "Your Way" section. Encourage people to read the participant's guide's "Tech Support" tips from Dr. Dobson as they try to balance love and control—and to read and complete the "Home Base," "Your Story," and "WordWorks" sections before your next meeting.

SESSION 5

TO SPANK OR
NOT TO SPANK

SESSION AIM
That group members will decide whether, when, and how to use corporal punishment in disciplining their children; and, if they choose to use it, that they will do so only in ways that benefit their children.

SCRIPTURES FOR STUDY
Proverbs 13:24; 23:13, 14; 29:15, 17

SETTING THE STAGE
• Before the session, group members should read and complete the following sections from chapter 5 of their participant's guides: "Home Base," "Your Story," and "WordWorks."
• Cue up the video to segment 5, "To Spank or Not to Spank."
• Gather the following items: pencils or pens, plus a paddle ball (see step 1).

STARTING OUT
It *is* possible—even easy—to create a violent and aggressive child who has observed [violent] behavior at home. If he is routinely beaten by hostile, volatile parents or if he witnesses physical violence between angry adults or if he feels unloved and unappreciated within his family,

that child will not fail to notice how the game is played. Thus, corporal punishment that is not administered according to very carefully thought-out guidelines is a risky thing. Being a parent carries no right to slap and intimidate a child because you had a bad day or are in a lousy mood. It is this kind of unjust discipline that causes some well-meaning authorities to reject corporal punishment as a method of discipline.

Just because a technique is used wrongly, however, is no reason to reject it altogether. Many children desperately need this resolution to their disobedience. In those situations when the child, aged two to ten, fully understands what he is being asked to do but refuses to yield to adult leadership, an appropriate spanking is the shortest and most effective route to an attitude adjustment. . . . There is not a single well-designed scientific study that confirms the hypothesis that spanking by a loving parent breeds violence in children.

—Dr. James Dobson in *The Complete Marriage and Family Home Reference Guide* (Tyndale House)

STEP 1

ALL IN THIS TOGETHER

(5-10 minutes)

Begin the meeting with this announcement:

Let's start this session with a little paddling.

Take out a paddle ball (a wooden paddle with an elastic band attached, to which is fastened a rubber ball) that you've brought. Ask for two volunteers; have them come up to the front.

Hand the paddle ball to one volunteer. Tell the second volunteer: **I'm going to ask you a question. While you answer, our first volunteer will hit the ball with the paddle. As long as he [or she] keeps hitting the ball, you keep answering.**

Chances are that the first volunteer won't be able to keep going for long, so the answer probably will be short. Thank your volunteers, then ask for two more and repeat the process with a new question. Here are questions from which to choose:

What's your reaction when you think of being spanked?
What's you reaction when you think of spanking a child?
When do you think it's good to spank a child?
When do you think it's bad to spank a child?
What was your most memorable spanking as you were growing up?
Are birthday spankings corporal punishment?

Would you ever spank your child in front of his or her friends?

After giving as many people as possible a chance to participate, introduce the session topic with comments like these:

Spanking is pretty controversial these days. In this session we'll explore whether or not corporal punishment can and should be an effective part of disciplining our children.

STEP 2

YOU ARE HERE

(5-10 minutes)

Have group members turn to the participant's guide section, "Your Story." Invite them to share their answers. After hearing the words people associated with the terms "corporal punishment" and "spanking," ask volunteers to tell why those words sprang to mind—if they know.

Since spanking is an especially sensitive subject, be prepared for the possibility of sharp disagreement among participants. Some may be reluctant to say anything, believing others would look down on their use of spanking (or opposition to it). Emphasize that these are primarily opinion questions, and that you're not looking for "right" answers.

If you think group members would be more comfortable sharing their opinions with just a partner, form pairs and allow them to do that.

Wrap up this section with a question like this: **What question about spanking do you most hope is answered in the video for this session? Why?**

STEP 3

SCREEN TIME

(15-30 minutes)

Pass out pencils or pens. Watch video segment 5, entitled, "To Spank or Not to Spank." Encourage group members to use the "Screen Time" section of the participant's guide for taking notes.

After watching the video segment, discuss it, using questions and comments like the following:

What's the actual meaning of the term, "corporal punishment"? (Bodily punishment, inflicting a physical penalty.)

Spanking used to be widely used as a discipline tool. Now it's controversial, even taboo in some societies. Why do you think that is? (Some may think it reflects a general trend to let kids "get away with" more; others may feel it's a reaction to child abuse.)

Before you viewed the video, what was your general feeling about spanking as a form of punishment?

Has your view changed after watching the video? Why or why not?

What reason did Dr. Dobson give for parental abuse or violence toward children? (When parents have no answer for misbehaivor.)

In each of the following situations, would you respond with a spanking, a slap on the hand, or another form of discipline? Why?

- Your two-year-old runs toward the street, and you catch him just in time.
- Your two-year-old runs toward the street, and you catch him just in time—and this is the third time it's happened today.
- You ask your six-year-old to pick up her toys, and she slams the door in your face.
- Your eight-year-old calls his sister a pig; you tell him to apologize, and he responds by telling her, "I'm sorry you're a pig."
- Your eleven-year-old refuses to take responsibility for feeding the cat, even though she was the one who wanted a pet.
- Your 13-year-old son is suspended from school for getting in a fight.

After listening to responses, ask:

What hints did the video offer about the proper administration of a spanking? (Reserve spankings for willful defiance; don't use excessive force; don't use spanking as a last resort; spank on the "behind" and consider using a "neutral" object instead of a hand.)

According to the video, who should not spank? (Those who have had a problem with child abuse, are out of control, or "enjoy" spanking; those who aren't the child's parent and don't have parental permission.)

What children should not be spanked? (Babies, teens, or those with certain special needs, and compliant children.)

STEP 4

BY THE BOOK

(5-10 minutes)

Ask group members to turn to the "WordWorks" section of this session in their participant's guides. Ask them to call out their answers to the questions that follow.

1. Proverbs 29:15

Why do you suppose correction is described as a "rod" here? (Some commentators believe this refers not to an instrument used for "beating," but to a staff used to persuade livestock to return to the right path. In the same way, discipline can persuade a child to correct his or her behavior.)

Do parents ever spank children for reasons other than correction? What might some of those reasons be? (Some parents spank when they've had a lousy day, or because they don't consider other ways to discipline, or because they enjoy inflicting punishment—all illegitimate reasons for spanking.)

According to this verse, what happens when parents don't correct their children? How might this look in real life? (Children who grow up without discipline end up disgracing their parents, in the words of this verse. That might look like a child in rebellion, or a child who has no healthy relationships, or a child who becomes an adult who has no self-discipline.)

2. Proverbs 13:24

Dr. Dobson writes that spanking is an appropriate method of discipline for many children in response to willful defiance. Does this seem like a loving response to you? Why or why not? (Answers will vary. Those affirming spanking might note that it can be a short and effective way to an attitude adjustment in the child. Those in opposition might feel it's too easy for a spanking to become abusive.)

Do you think most parents today would agree with this verse? Why or why not? (Perhaps most parents in Western societies today would disagree, depending on what they thought the "rod" represents. Encourage participants to respond in the context of your community.)

3. Proverbs 23:13, 14

How might a parent misuse this passage to try to justify child abuse? (He or she might wrongly claim that because saving a soul is more important that sparing the physical body, a child may be physically punished to a point just short of death.)

How could spanking be more merciful than *not* spanking? Can you give a real-life example? (Some possibilities: when a child is headed toward a dangerous situation, such as sticking a screwdriver into an electrical outlet, or ignoring your calls as she walks from your lawn onto a busy street; or when a child commits antisocial acts that will alienate others or lead to criminal behavior.)

4. PROVERBS 29:17

How could a careful use of spanking bring peace and delight to a parent's relationship with a child? Have you ever seen this happen? (When the appropriate use of spanking establishes early on that the parent is in charge, repeated challenges to parental authority and the stress that goes with them may be avoided or at least reduced—and the child may feel more secure because boundaries are enforced.)

STEP 5

WORK IT OUT

(10 minutes)

Have group members flip to the "Your Way" section of their participant's guides. Give people at least five minutes to complete the activities. Let married couples work together; to avoid isolating single parents, however, have singles work along with couples. If time is limited, have group members concentrate on item 3, the "Corporal Punishment Code," and leave the rest for later.

Wrap up the session as follows:

It's possible for parents to rely too heavily on spanking—and other forms of punishment, for that matter. Dr. Dobson has some thoughts on that subject in *The Complete Marriage and Family Home Reference Guide* (Tyndale House):

"Without watering down anything I have written about discipline, it should be understood that I am a firm believer in the judicious use of grace (and humor) in parent-child relationships. In a world in which children are often pushed to grow up too fast, their spirits can dry out like prunes beneath the constant gaze of critical eyes. It is refreshing to see parents temper their harshness with a measure of 'unmerited favor.' Likewise, there's nothing that buoys every member of a family quite like laughter and a lighthearted spirit in the home."

Close by asking people to pray silently, committing their Corporal Punishment Codes to the Lord, asking Him to help them as they seek to guide their children with love and consistent discipline.

Remind group members to look over the "Tech Support" tips

from Dr. Dobson included in their participant's guides, which may answer some questions as they apply what they've learned. Also urge them to read and complete the "Home Base," "Your Story," and "WordWorks" sections before your next meeting.

SESSION 6

Compliant Cleve   *And*   Strong-Willed Steve

COMPLIANT VS. DEFIANT

SESSION AIM   To help group members determine whether their children are compliant or defiant, and to provide concrete ideas on parenting both kinds of children.

SCRIPTURES FOR STUDY   Matthew 21:28-31; Genesis 4:1-7

SETTING THE STAGE
- Before the session, participants should read and complete these sections in chapter 6 of their participant's guides: "Home Base," "Your Story," and "WordWorks."
- Cue up the video to segment 6, "Compliant vs. Defiant"
- You'll also need pens or pencils; signs that read, "Strong-willed" and "Compliant"; tape or other means to fasten the signs to the walls of your meeting place; and two sets of "Scenario Cards" copied and cut from step 1.

STARTING OUT   Most parents have at least one [strong-willed child] who seems to be born with a clear idea of how he wants the world to be operated and an intolerance for those who disagree. Even in infancy, he fairly bristles when his dinner is late and he insists that someone hold him during every waking hour. Later, during toddlerhood he declares total war on all forms of authority, at home or abroad, and his greatest thrill comes from drawing on the walls and flushing kitties down the toilet. His parents are often guilt-ridden and frustrated people who wonder where they've gone wrong and why their home life is so different than they were led to expect. . . .

It is my firm conviction that the strong-willed child usually possesses more creative potential and strength of character than his compliant siblings, provided his parents can help him channel his impulses and gain control of his rampaging will.

—Dr. James Dobson in *The Strong-Willed Child* (Tyndale House)

Step 1

All in This Together

(5-10 minutes)

Before the session, make two signs. One should say, "Strong-willed"; the other should say "Compliant." Hang the signs on opposite walls in your meeting place. Then start the session with this group-building activity.

Ask people to gather under one sign or the other, according to whether they think *they* were strong-willed or compliant as kids. (If everyone gathers under the same sign, ask a few volunteers to fill in under the other one.) Give one person in each group a copy of each of the following "Scenario Cards":

The cardholder in each group should read the first scenario aloud. Each group should decide how it would have responded to the situation. As time allows, have the groups do the same with the other two scenarios; then have them share results with each other.

SCENARIO 1

You're six years old, hiking with Mom and Dad in a national park. They keep telling you not to get too far ahead. You look up at a ridge close to you and notice a mountain goat. It's so near, you can almost reach out and touch it. In fact, with just a little climbing, you could. What do you do?

> **SCENARIO 2**
> You're eleven years old. You have your first serious crush on someone of the opposite sex. Your parents are being nice about it, but when you ask to go to the movies with this person, your parents say you're too young. How do you respond?

> **SCENARIO 3**
> There's a new kid at school. This person is very different from your other friends. Your parents think this person is "trouble waiting to happen." You're 17, but your parents still ask you not to hang around with this kid anymore. Your response?

Don't worry if there's disagreement, or if you don't get through all three scenarios. It's most important that people get talking about how the mind of a strong-willed or compliant child works. Then say something like this:

Strong-willed and compliant children can look at things so differently that they often have a hard time understanding how "the other half" thinks. As parents, we can have a hard time understanding, too. In this session let's look at these two types of children and how to parent each successfully.

Before moving to the next step, invite group members to sit wherever they'd like—regardless of their personality types.

STEP 2
YOU ARE HERE

(5-10 minutes)

Ask people to turn in their participant's guides to the section titled, "Your Story." Have them share answers to the degree that they're willing. If you think it would help group members to open up, form pairs for discussion instead of trying to discuss as a whole group.

You may want to define terms. Here are some comments to share:

The compliant child is one who, due to his or her basic temperament, usually cooperates with parents and other authority figures.

The defiant (or strong-willed) child is one who, due to his or her basic temperament, is more demanding and uncooperative.

Our purpose here isn't to brand compliant kids as "good" and strong-willed kids as "bad." As you think about your childhood and about which categories your own children fall into, rest assured that it's okay to be or have either type.

After discussing "Your Story" responses, wrap up this step with the following question: **As you think of your strong-willed and compliant children, what do you most hope to gain from today's video segment?**

STEP 3

SCREEN TIME

(15-30 minutes)

Together with your group, watch segment 6 of the video, titled, "Compliant vs. Defiant?" Make sure all who need one have a pencil or pen with which to take notes in their participant's guide section, "Screen Time."

When the video segment is over, discuss it with the group, using questions and comments similar to these:

Remember Compliant Cleve and Strong-willed Steve? Which kid lives at your house? Or do they both?

What do you think will happen in the "exciting season finale" of the *Compliant Cleve and Strong-willed Steve* **show?**

Did any of the battles mentioned in this video remind you of battles you've faced at home? If so, which ones? How did you handle them?

Have you ever felt like the residents of the Home for Parents of Strong-willed Children? When?

Dr. Dobson has said, "Even the toughest kids find security in a structured environment where the rights of other people, as well as their own, are protected." If you have both strong-willed and compliant children, have you been able to protect the rights of both? What's your biggest challenge in this area?

Which of the following statistics from the video is most encouraging to you? Why?

- There are nearly three times as many strong-willed children as compliant ones.

- Most strong-willed children show a rapid decrease in rebellious behavior when they hit young adulthood.
- 85 percent of strong-willed kids tend to return to the values of their parents when they become adults.

Point out that in upcoming sessions, you'll be exploring more specific ways to deal with the wills of strong-willed kids.

Step 4

By the Book

(5-10 minutes)

Ask your group to turn to the "WordWorks" Bible study for this session. Encourage people to call out their answers in response to the questions that follow.

1. Matthew 21:28-31

In the above story told by Jesus, do you think either of the sons was compliant? Defiant? Why? (Answers may vary; in the beginning, though, it seemed the first son was defiant and the second compliant. But their actions proved them to be the opposite—leading one to wonder whether the first son was compliant but testing boundaries.)

Would you call either son a "strong-willed child"? Why or why not? (Answers will vary. It seems the second son was more passively defiant, and possibly more strong-willed. On the other hand, some strong-willed children say no to a request at first but decide to act on it later.)

Suppose the father, before the events of the story, had labeled the first son as defiant and the second as compliant. Would the events have changed his mind? Why or why not? Opinions may vary. As needed, you may want to point out that labels are less important than behavior. In fact, labeling one child as "uncooperative" and another as "obedient" can lead to unfair treatment and worsen sibling rivalry.

How do you think the father should deal with the sons' responses to his direction? (Answers will vary. Perhaps the father should talk with the sons about the fact that obedient actions are far more valuable than obedient words.)

2. Genesis 4:1-7

Cain brought "some" of his produce as an offering; Abel brought the *best* of his flock. How might their actions indicate compliance or

defiance? (Cain seemed to be doing as little as possible to get by, which could indicate defiance; Abel was doing his best to please God, which probably indicates compliance.)

How did being strong-willed seem to affect Cain's response to God's correction? (Cain wasn't happy at all about being corrected; he became sullen and depressed when corrected; he wanted to justify his behavior rather than take care of the problems his attitude and actions were causing.)

In your experience, how does a strong-willed child tend to react to advice or criticism? (Group members' experiences may vary, but strong-willed children often respond negatively to correction.)

Why might the parent of a strong-willed child be reluctant to correct or discipline him or her? (Some parents might feel that dealing with the negative response of a strong-willed child after discipline is worse than actually disciplining the child.)

What might be the result of failing to discipline a strong-willed child? (A lack of discipline could result in the defiant child rejecting all authority.)

STEP 5

WORK IT OUT

(10 minutes)

Instruct the group to turn to the "Your Way" section in the participant's guide. Give people at least five minutes to work thorough the activities individually. If time is short, have group members address the first two items and leave the rest for later.

If time allows, let volunteers share the results of their work.

Before closing, you may wish to encourage parents of strong-willed children with the following story from Dr. Dobson's book *The Complete Marriage and Family Home Reference Guide* (Tyndale House):

"**[Five-year-old Laura] was observed by her father to have become especially disobedient and defiant. She was irritating other family members and looking for ways to avoid minding her parents. Her dad decided not to confront her directly but to punish her consistently for every offense until she settled down. Thus, for three or four days, he let Laura get away with nothing. . . . Near the end of the fourth day, she was sitting on the bed with her father and younger sister. Without provocation, Laura pulled the hair of the toddler, who was looking at a book. Her dad promptly thumped her on the head with his large hand. Laura did not cry but sat in silence** for a moment or two and then said, 'Harumph! All my tricks are not working!'

"This is the conclusion you want your strong-willed [child] to draw: 'It's too risky to take on Mom or Dad, so let's get with the program.'"

Close by praying for your group members, asking the Lord to help them match their parenting methods to their children's temperaments. Remind people to read the "Tech Support" tips in the participant's guide to help them stay on track in meeting their goals—and to read and complete the "Home Base," "Your Story," and "WordWorks" sections before your next meeting.

SESSION 7

B) When Your Child Finally Drives You Crazy

CHANGING DISCIPLINE AS YOUR CHILD GROWS, PART 1

SESSION AIM   To help group members match disciplinary methods to the maturity levels of young children.

SCRIPTURES FOR STUDY   Proverbs 12:1; 15:32; 22:6; 1 Timothy 3:4

SETTING THE STAGE
- Before the session, participants should read and complete these sections in chapter 7 of their participant's guides: "Home Base," "Your Story," and "WordWorks."
- Cue up the video to segment 7, "Changing Discipline as Your Child Grows, Part 1."
- You'll need pens or pencils; chalkboard and chalk or other display surface and writing tool; and materials for the activity in the "All in This Together" section (see step 1).

STARTING OUT   Many of the spankings and slaps given to toddlers can and should be avoided. Toddlers get in trouble most frequently because of their natural desire to touch, bite, taste, smell, and break everything within their grasp. However, this exploratory behavior is not aggressive. It is a valuable means for learning and should not be discouraged. I have seen parents slap their two-year-olds throughout the day for simply investigating their world. This squelching of normal curiosity is not fair to the youngster.

When, then, should the toddler be subjected to mild discipline? When he openly defies his parents' spoken commands! . . . The toddler years are critical to a child's future attitude toward authority. He should be taught to patiently obey without being expected to behave like a more mature child.

—Dr. James Dobson in *The New Strong-Willed Child*

STEP 1

ALL IN THIS TOGETHER

(5-10 minutes)

In this session you'll be talking about keeping discipline age appropriate. A baby or toddler is discovering the world for the first time. They use their senses—taste, sight, smell, sound, touch—in order to learn. To show the importance of patience and control during the "exploratory" years, start by involving volunteers from your group in a little "learning" experience.

Blindfold two volunteers and bring in a few different containers of items and place them on a table in front of them. Instruct the explorers to reach their hand in the container and discern what is inside. They can roll their hands in it, smell it, listen to the sound it makes to discover what the substance or item is.

Be as challenging or as creative as you can with the items you choose for this activity. Below are suggestions to get you started. Use as many or as few as time allows.

- A bowl of potpourri
- Wet prunes
- Mustard seeds
- Jelly
- Crushed shells, sea or nut
- Dry (or wet) spaghetti

STEP 2

YOU ARE HERE

(5-10 minutes)

Have group members flip to the "Your Story" section in their participant's guides. Since some of the exercises involve visual responses, form pairs or small groups so that people can see each other's drawings. If time is short, have participants concentrate on questions 1 and 5.

As needed, comment along the following lines in order to help the discussion along.

Item 1

Don't worry if you can't manage a Norman Rockwell family portrait. The important thing is to consider whether discipline has had an unexpected effect on your family.

Item 2

You can interpret the shapes any way you like; just explain your interpretation to the rest of your group.

Item 3

Remember that disciplining a child goes beyond just controlling behavior. It's also an inside job, working on a child's attitude toward authority.

Item 4

For example, will you need a tool that rubs away rough spots? One that makes the "clay" softer in order to be molded?

Item 5

If you have no fears about disciplining your child, that's fine. But if you have concerns or questions, feel free to share those.

STEP 3

SCREEN TIME

(15-30 minutes)

Watch video segment 7, "Changing Discipline as Your Child Grows, Part 1." Make pencils or pens available to your group, and encourage people to take notes in the "Screen Time" section of the participant's guide.

After viewing the video segment, discuss it together using questions and comments like the following.

What are some important things to remember from the video when it comes to disciplining your child during the babyhood and toddler years?

Infants (birth to 7 months)? (No direct discipline; instill emotional and physical health through security, affection, and warmth.)

Babies (8-14 months)? (Discipline needs to be very gentle: no spanking or shaking; distract little ones from troublesome behavior, establishing authority—loving leadership is the goal.)

Toddlers? (Don't punish exploration, but deal with defiance through persistence, time outs, and controlled corporal punishment; set boundaries that put dangerous behavior off limits.)

2-3 years? (Keep a sense of humor, instill obedience and a respect for authority.)

After watching the video, is it ever a good idea to "reason" with a toddler? Why not? Are there any adjustments you'd like to make in the discipline techniques you're using? Why?

STEP 4

BY THE BOOK

(5-10 minutes)

Ask the group to turn to the "WordWorks" Bible study section for this session. Encourage group members to call out their answers to the questions that follow.

1. 1 TIMOTHY 3:4
What do you think a well-managed family looks like? (Some possibilities: Children aren't out of control; parents are the leaders, but not oppressors; a genuine love within the family can be sensed by those around them, etc.)

How can you tell when your children are obeying you with "proper respect?" Answers will vary. As needed, point out that respect indicates a healthy attitude toward authority, not just outward conformity to rules. A parent who's truly respected by his or her children would not be a tyrant, even though a tyrant might be able to exact obedience that would "look good" to the outside world.

Do these two goals seem achievable to you? Why or why not? (People may say yes because they think it's the "right" answer, but encourage them to be honest about misgivings they may have. Parents with strong-willed children face special challenges in meeting these goals.)

2. PROVERBS 15:32; 12:1
If you had to convince a strong-willed child of the truth of these verses, how would you do it? (One option might be to help the child

see how correction—fixing a mistake—benefits him or her. It can keep a person out of danger, improve a skill, and save time and effort.)

3. PROVERBS 22:6

What's the value of appropriate discipline early in life? (Children are more flexible and trainable then; they're more likely to see the parent as the authority; they'll waste less time in rebellion.)

Note: It's possible that some group members may wonder why, in light of Proverbs 22:6, some children "go wrong" when their parents seem to have trained them well. While this is an important issue, you'll want to avoid sidetracking the discussion in that direction. The issue of "prodigal" children is addressed in another course in this series. For now, you may want to acknowledge that many parents have assumed Proverbs 22:6 is a guarantee that well-trained children will stay on the "straight and narrow." But biblical proverbs are more accurately taken as statements of principles that are generally true—not as promises.

Do you wish someone had done more to teach you discipline you when you were growing up? Why or why not? Allow volunteers to share their answers as time allows.

STEP 5

WORK IT OUT

(10 minutes)

Have the group turn to the "Your Way" section in the participant's guide. Give everyone at least five minutes to answer the questions. If time allows, ask volunteers to share some of their "battle plans." If there's disagreement over which confrontations are worth pursuing, don't worry; just ask people to explain their answers.

Close the session by asking the group to pray for all of the children who are in group members' homes. Ask for guidance and perseverance in gently disciplining these children.

Remind group members to look over the "Tech Support" tips from Dr. Dobson included in their participant's guides, which may answer some questions as they apply what they've learned. Also urge them to read and complete the next "Home Base," "Your Story," and "WordWorks" sections before your next meeting.

SESSION 8

A) To Be Sure Your Child Is Seen And Not Heard

CHANGING DISCIPLINE AS YOUR CHILD GROWS, PART 2

SESSION AIM
To help group members match disciplinary methods to the ages and maturity levels of their children.

SCRIPTURES FOR STUDY
Ecclesiastes 3:1-8; 1 Corinthians 13:11; Ephesians 4:2

SETTING THE STAGE
- Before the session, participants should read and complete these sections in chapter 8 of their participant's guides: "Home Base," "Your Story," and "WordWorks."
- Cue up the video to segment 8, "Changing Discipline as Your Child Grows, Part 2."
- You'll also need pens or pencils; chalkboard and chalk or other display surface and writing tool; and materials for the "childish" activities you choose in the "All in This Together" section (see step 1).

STARTING OUT
The wise parent must understand the physical and emotional characteristics of each stage in childhood, and then fit the discipline to a

boy's or girl's individual needs. . . .

Ideally, the foundation has been laid during the first nine years which will then permit a general loosening of the lines of authority. Every year that passes should bring fewer rules, less direct discipline, and more independence for the child. This does not mean that a ten-year-old is suddenly emancipated; it does mean that he is permitted to make more decisions about his daily living than when he was six. It also means that he should be carrying more responsibility each year of his life. . . .

My concept is that parents should introduce their child to discipline and self-control by the use of external influences when he is young. By being required to behave responsibly, he gains valuable experience in controlling his *own* impulses and resources.

—Dr. James Dobson in *The New Dare to Discipline* (Tyndale House)

STEP I

ALL IN THIS TOGETHER

(5-10 minutes)

In this session you'll be talking about keeping discipline age-appropriate. To show the importance of treating people according to their maturity level, start by engaging in some age-*inappropriate* behavior—treating your group members like children.

Depending on the time you have to prepare and your willingness to do a little acting, you can go all-out with this idea—or just try one or two of the following suggestions:

- When you greet people as they arrive, use baby talk (for example, "Ooh, and did you have a good widdle week?")
- Call group members by the diminutive versions of their names ("Johnny," "Paulie," "Chrissie," etc.).
- Serve "childish" refreshments like baby food on crackers.
- Ask volunteers to play a game like "Ring Around the Rosie."
- Offer group members teething biscuits as rewards for "good behavior."
- Pick someone who's talking out of turn and send him or her to sit in the corner. (Note: You may want to arrange this in advance to avoid embarrassing the victim.)
- Talk "down" to the group (for instance, "Our topic today is probably too complicated for you to understand, but I'll try not to use any big words").

- Issue a list of "class rules" ("Raise your hand if you have to use the bathroom," "No fidgeting," etc.).
- Try to get the group to sing a song like "Climb, Climb up Sunshine Mountain" or "Deep and Wide," using the motions.
- Announce that you're going to do a craft project using paper plates, cotton balls, and pipe cleaners.

After a few minutes of this, explain that you haven't lost your mind. Ask: **How does it feel to be treated like a child?** (Some may find it amusing, but probably wouldn't put up with it for long.)

You've grown up. It doesn't make sense to pretend you haven't. The same is true of our kids; they change as they grow, and the way we discipline them has to change, too. That's what we'll be talking about today.

STEP 2

YOU ARE HERE

(5-10 minutes)

Instruct group members to turn in their participant's guides to the "Your Story" section for this session.

On the chalkboard or other display surface, draw a "timeline" from left to right. Make marks along the line to indicate age 1, age 2, etc., up to age 18. You'll be using this timeline to record group responses.

As you discuss the words and phrases people chose for various childhood stages in Item 1, write some of them along the timeline at the appropriate points. Don't worry if people associate the same word or phrase with different ages. There are no "right" answers in this exercise.

Then ask: **Do you find yourself using some of these words, phrases, or disciplinary methods when they might no longer be appropriate? Before they're appropriate?**

When it comes to discipline, is it likely that your kids are thinking any of these thoughts (such as, "Quit treating me like a baby!")?

If parents are reluctant to respond to these questions, just have them think about the issues.

What does this exercise tell you about the relationship between discipline and growing up? Answers will vary. As needed, point out that what works at one age won't at another. Yet it's not unusual for parents' perceptions of their kids' maturity to lag behind, or leap ahead of, reality.

As you discuss Items 2 and 3, let volunteers come up to your timeline and mark their responses—starting and stopping ages for discipline, and the ages at which certain disciplinary tactics work best.

STEP 3

SCREEN TIME

(15-30 minutes)   Watch video segment 8, "Changing Discipline as Your Child Grows, Part 2." Make pencils or pens available to your group, and encourage people to take notes in the "Screen Time" section of the participant's guide.

After viewing the video segment, discuss it together using questions and comments like the following.

When should parents begin focusing on the attitudes behind their children's behavior?

What are some other things to remember from the video regarding discipline of children aged 4-8? (Beginning at age four, focus not only on behavior but the attitudes behind it; model and teach biblical attitudes; there should be fewer rules and less direct discipline as the child matures. Attitudes are not consistent at this stage. Children of this age will learn what they are taught.)

What are some things to remember from the video reguarding discipline of children aged 9-12? (Discipline for older children should involve lost privileges, financial deprivation, and other kinds of non-physical penalties.)

What were Dr. Dobson's two "age-old" recommendations for shaping the attitudes of children? (Model the attitudes you wish to teach, and live the Judeo-Christian ethic.)

STEP 4

BY THE BOOK

(5-10 minutes)   Ask the group to turn to the "WordWorks" Bible study section for this session. Encourage group members to call out their answers to the questions that follow.

1. ECCLESIASTES 3:1-8
According to these verses, different times call for different responses. When it comes to disciplining your child(ren), how could it be right at one time to "tear down" and right at another to "build"? (Even within a single incident of discipline, you first correct and then reassure; there are some offenses that call for swift and certain parental action, and others that call for a child to endure the natural

consequences of his or her action; if punishment is a "tearing down" of misbehavior, setting boundaries proactively could be seen as "building.")

How could it be right at one time to "be silent" and right at another to "speak"? (Sometimes a parent needs to take time to control his or her anger, so silence is better until that point of control is reached; sometimes ignoring misbehavior extinguishes it [see session 7].)

How could it be right at one time to "embrace" and right at another to "refrain"? (A child needs to be assured of a parent's love as part of the disciplinary process, but the "embracing" usually takes place after the penalty is administered.)

How is disciplining an eight-year-old different from disciplining a sixteen-year-old? Try working as many phrases from the Ecclesiastes verses into your answer as you can. (There are numerous possibilities your group members could offer. Examples: elementary age might be a time to "plant" concepts of right and wrong, while adolescence might call for a parent to "uproot" harmful notions that peers have introduced.)

2. 1 CORINTHIANS 13:11

What could happen to a child whose parents discipline him without taking his changing mind and body into account? (Disciplinary tactics may become ineffective, even insulting.)

Did your parents, in their approach to disciplining you, seem to realize the truth of this verse? Why or why not? Answers will vary; some may be reluctant to reply. Empathize with any who describe childhoods marked by inappropriate discipline.

3. EPHESIANS 4:2

Do you think it takes more patience to discipline a five-year-old or a teenager? Why?

Which of the aforementioned qualities—humility, gentleness, patience, or love—do you need most to help you cope with the changes occurring in your child(ren)? As needed, point out that humility may help us to be more observant of our children's needs and maturity levels; gentleness may help us ease up on a youngster who's entering the turbulence of adolescence; patience could get us through the rough spots; love might help us to put our children's need for age-appropriate discipline before our own convenience in disciplining "the way we've always done it.")

STEP 5

WORK IT OUT

(10 minutes)

Have the group turn to the "Your Way" section in the participant's guide. Give people at least five minutes to work through the activities individually.

Before closing, you may want to comment along the following lines:

There's no doubt that our disciplinary methods need to keep up with our children's maturity levels. But there are some things about discipline that stay the same. We touched on these in an earlier session, but here's a reminder of six disciplinary principles that are true at any age, adapted from Dr. Dobson's book *The Complete Marriage and Family Home Reference Guide* (Tyndale House):

First: Define the boundaries before they're enforced.

Second: When defiantly challenged, respond with confident decisiveness.

Third: Distinguish between willful defiance and childish irresponsibility.

Fourth: Reassure and teach as soon as the confrontation is over.

Fifth: Avoid impossible demands.

Sixth: Let love be your guide.

Remind group members to read the "Tech Support" section in the participant's guide for parenting hints they can put into practice—and to read and complete the next "Home Base," "Your Story," and "WordWorks" sections before you meet again.

SESSION 9

PROTECTING THE SPIRIT

SESSION AIM To help group members discover and use ways to shape a child's will without damaging his or her sense of personal worth.

SCRIPTURES FOR STUDY Ephesians 6:4; Proverbs 17:26; Malachi 4:6

SETTING THE STAGE • Before the session, group members should read and complete these sections in chapter 9 of their participant's guides: "Home Base," "Your Story," and "WordWorks."
• Cue up the video to segment 9, "Protecting the Spirit."
• You'll also need pens or pencils; a large, resealable, clear plastic bag; several cookies; a hammer; a bowl; and a copy of the Situation Slips (see "All in This Together").

STARTING OUT Dick Korthals, one of our volunteers here at Focus on the Family, tells of an experience he had while attending a dog show.

　　As part of the competition, about a dozen dogs were commanded to "Stay!" and then expected to remain in a statue-like manner for eight minutes while their owners left the ring. Judges scored them on how well they were able to hold their composure during their master's absence.

Well, about four minutes into the exercise, Dick noticed the dog on the end, a magnificent German Shepherd named Jake. He seemed to be losing his poise, slinking slowly toward the ground. By the time his trainer returned, poor Jake was lying flat on his stomach with his head on his paws. Now Jake immediately saw the disappointment in his owner's eyes and began crawling on his belly toward him. Everyone was expecting the trainer to scold the dog for his poor performance. But instead, he bent down and he cupped the dog's head in his hands, and then he said with a smile, "That's okay, Jake. We'll do better next time." It was a very touching moment. There's a lesson here for every parent, too.

Children are going to disappoint us. It's an inevitable part of child-rearing. And when they do, our natural reaction is to bark at them, "Why'd you do that?" and, "How could you have been so stupid?" But if we're wise, we'll remember that they're just immature children, just like we used to be, and simply say with warmth, "That's okay. You'll do better next time."

—Dr. James Dobson

STEP 1

ALL IN THIS TOGETHER

(5-10 minutes)

Before the session, put several cookies in a resealable, clear plastic bag. Copy and cut out the "Situation Slips" that follow. Put the slips in a bowl. You'll need to bring a hammer, too.

Start your session with comments like these:

You might call our opening activity "That's the Way the Cookie Crumbles."

Hold up the bag of cookies.

Here are some perfectly yummy cookies. But cookies are fragile. We have to be careful to treat them gently or all we'll have is a pile of crumbs.

Let four volunteers choose "Situation Slips" from the bowl. Then say: **Our volunteers are going to read four very short stories. After each story, we'll vote on whether the spirits of the children in the stories are likely to be crushed by what the parent did.**

Have the first volunteer read his or her story. Here are the slips:

Mom and Dad have just finished painting the trim on the house and gone inside to rest. Eight-year-old Stephen decides to help by watering the garden. He does well at first, but then loses interest. As he looks around distractedly, he sprays the house, causing the paint to run onto the patio. Mom rolls open the patio door and shouts at Stephen, "What do you think you're doing? You know better than that! How could you be so stupid?"

Alice and her friend Brittany, ages five and six, have been playing with dolls all day. Now there's a wide trail of doll accessories throughout the house. Coming out of the laundry room, Mom trips over a doll's "dream house" and falls into her favorite lamp, breaking it. Seething, she rounds up the girls and orders them to pick up everything on the floor, right down to the pieces of cat hair on the carpet. She also bans all doll-playing for a week.

Dad is ready to take 11-year-old twins Carter and Matthew on a long-planned camping trip tomorrow. But the closer it gets, the worse the boys seem to behave—arguing with each other about everything. Dad finally yells, "That's it! You obviously don't want to go camping, so forget it!" The boys try to apologize to Dad. But he's too angry to talk.

Dad and Mom are in great need of a date. It seems like half a lifetime since they've been alone. Dad asks their teenager Jenny to watch her siblings one Friday night. Jenny responds that she wanted to borrow the car and see a movie with her friends. Dad, his blood pressure rising, says through gritted teeth, "It's my car. I'm tired of having to stand in line for it. You'll just have to postpone your movie. I don't think that will kill you, will it?"

After the first story is read, have the group vote on whether the parent's action would crush the child's spirit. If the vote is an overwhelming yes, use the hammer to deliver a crushing blow to the cookies in the bag. If just a few people vote yes, give the cookies a firm but less devastating blow. Then ask how the parent might have handled the situation without "crushing" the child.

Repeat the process with the other three stories—or as many of them as time allows. Then hold up the bag of cookies again.

Kind of hard to put these back together, huh? It's the same way with kids. Sometimes in the process of trying to shape the wills of our children, we end up crushing their spirits. Today we'll look at ways to keep our kids' spirits intact.

STEP 2

YOU ARE HERE

(5-10 minutes)

Call group members' attention to the "Your Story" section in the participant's guide. Invite them to share their responses if they're willing.

If you sense that group members won't want to reveal answers, perhaps because they'd put themselves or their parents in a bad light, try a different approach. Fill out the "Your Story" section yourself before the session, and share your own responses at this time. If that encourages others to talk about their own experiences, fine. If not, let the group discuss your answers and talk about how parents in general often find themselves yelling at their children or failing to listen to them.

STEP 3

SCREEN TIME

(15-30 minutes)

Show video segment 9, "Protecting the Spirit." Make pens or pencils available to any group member who needs one for note taking in the "Screen Time" section of the participant's guide.

After viewing the video segment, discuss it with the group using questions and comments like the following:

Have you ever felt like the sculptor in the first cartoon? You may want to remind the group that in the first sequence the sculptor hit his chisel and the statue collapsed.

How can you tell when something you've done or said has "shattered" your child?

Is it fair to expect a parent to stifle an angry reaction in order to spare a child's feelings? Opinions may vary. As needed, note that parents have a right to their emotions, too. But it's important to express those emotions in a way that doesn't attack a child's worth.

What are some things a parent could say to a child to express displeasure without attacking the child? (Examples: "I know you'll try to do better next quarter. To help, you should plan to spend another half hour a day studying." "You have to treat your little brother with more respect. No more name calling." "I expect you to use proper manners when we get back to the table. Have I made myself clear?")

What role does consistency play when you're shaping your child's will? (It ensures that the child feels secure.)

According to Dr. Dobson, the goal of dealing with a difficult child is to shape the will without breaking the spirit. As a parent, how do you make the distinction between the will and the spirit? Allow opinions, but note that Dr. Dobson defines the difference in terms of strength and sensitivity.

Step 4

By the Book

(5-10 minutes)

Have your group turn in their participant's guides to the "Word-Works" Bible study section.

1. Ephesians 6:4

This teaching from the Bible can fit moms and dads alike. So think about this: In what ways might you exasperate your children? It's hard to see one's own shortcomings, but encourage parents to imagine their children's perspective. Kids might be exasperated by nagging, harshness, a failure to listen to their side, unfairness, inconsistency, or parents who don't "practice what they preach."

This verse implies that it's possible to train and instruct kids without exasperating them. What were some other ways you came up with to do that? (Other ideas: being gentle; speaking calmly; allowing kids to be imperfect; admitting mistakes and apologizing; not telling the same stories over and over about "when I was your age"; modeling the behavior you're teaching; using "teachable moments" instead of lecturing.)

2. PROVERBS 17:26

Were you ever unjustly corrected or punished? What were your feelings at that moment? Group members who are willing to reply may recall feelings of frustration, outrage, or powerlessness.

Do you think your children ever feel unjustly corrected or punished? How do you help them deal with those feelings? Almost every child feels some correction or punishment was unwarranted. As needed, note that parents can help by listening to their children's feelings, explaining the boundaries again, and talking about how to prevent misunderstandings in the future.

3. MALACHI 4:6

Do you see this happening in your family? In your country? In the world?

How could protecting the spirits of our children help to reach this goal? (Children with healthy self-images are better able to empathize with others, including parents. Kids whose spirits are crushed may try to protect themselves from further damage by withdrawing, rebelling, or becoming defensive or self-centered.)

STEP 5

WORK IT OUT

(10 minutes)

Turn with the group to the "Your Way" section in the participant's guide. Give people at least five minutes to work through the activities individually. If time is short, have participants concentrate on questions 2 and 3 and leave the rest for later.

If time allows, divide the group into couples or teams and let volunteers share any answers they feel are not too personal.

Before closing your session, point out that even if children seem to be obedient now, the effects of "breaking the spirit" can show up in the future. Share the following warning by Dr. Dobson, taken from *The New Dare to Discipline* (Tyndale House):

"A father who is sarcastic and biting in his criticism of children cannot expect to receive genuine respect in return. His offspring might *fear* him enough to conceal their contempt. But revenge will often be sought in adolescence. Children know the wisdom of the old axiom, 'Don't mock the alligator until you are across the stream.' Thus, a vicious, toothy father may intimidate his household for a time, but if he does not demonstrate respect for its inhabitants, they may return his hostility when they reach the safety of early adulthood."

Close by having volunteers pray about the goals they've set. Remind group members to read the "Tech Support" section in the participant's guide for parenting hints they can put into practice—and to read and complete the next "Home Base," "Your Story," and "WordWorks" sections before you meet again.

SESSION 10

THE STRONG-WILLED ADOLESCENT, PART 1

SESSION AIM

To help group members meet the unique challenge of disciplining strong-willed adolescents.

SCRIPTURES FOR STUDY

Luke 2:41-51; 1 Samuel 17:32-40, 50

SETTING THE STAGE

• Before the session, group members should read and complete these sections in chapter 10 of their participant's guides: "Home Base," "Your Story," and "WordWorks."

• Cue up the video to segment 10, "The Strong-Willed Adolescent, Part 1."

• You'll also need pens or pencils, plus supplies for any of the "Willpower Olympics" activities you choose (see step 1).

STARTING OUT

Alas, we arrive now at the door of adolescence: that dynamic time of life which comes in with a pimple and goes out with a beard. . . . It's an exciting phase of childhood, I suppose, but to be honest, I wouldn't want to stumble through it again. I doubt that the reader would either. We adults remember all too clearly the fears and jeers and tears that represented our own tumultuous youth. Perhaps that is why parents begin to quake and tremble when their children approach the adolescent years. . . .

—Dr. James Dobson in *The New Strong-Willed Child*
(Tyndale House)

STEP 1

ALL IN THIS TOGETHER

(5-10 minutes)

Start the session by staging a "Willpower Olympics." Depending on the time available, choose one or more of the following contests:

- Challenge volunteers to speak, without pausing, for 30 seconds on the subject of "My Summer Vacation." The catch is that the speakers must resist the temptation to use the word "I." See how many speakers can go the full 30 seconds.
- Bring a squirt gun. Have a group member (with whom you've arranged this beforehand) sit at the front of the room. Offer three volunteers a dollar apiece if they'll squirt the person. See whether they can resist.

After having fun with one or both of these stunts, make the transition to this session's topic:

So, who's the strongest-willed person in our group?

What age level do you think is more strong-willed—two-year-olds or teenagers? Why?

Many parents of teenagers probably would say that adolescents are the strongest-willed kids of all. They certainly pose special challenges. Figuring out how to handle discipline with strong-willed teenagers is the topic of our discussion today.

STEP 2

YOU ARE HERE

(5-10 minutes)

Form two groups—those who currently are raising teenagers (Group 1), and those who may someday raise teenagers (Group 2). Direct both groups to the "Your Story" section in their participant's guides. Have Group 1 discuss its answers to Items 1 and 2. Group 2 should talk over its replies to Items 1 and 3.

Then bring the whole group back together. Ask:

Are the memories of your own teen years getting fuzzy?

When you recall what it was like to be a teenager, what word best describes the feelings that come back to you?

Next, take a vote on the validity of the statement in Item 4, "All teenagers are strong-willed." Let volunteers explain their answers.

Wrap up this section by asking for a show of hands on the following question: **How many of you were strong-willed when *you* were a teenager?**

STEP 3

SCREEN TIME

(15-30 minutes)

Play video segment 10, entitled, "The Strong-Willed Adolescent, Part 1." Make pencils or pens available for taking notes in the "Screen Time" section of the participant's guide.

After watching the video segment together, discuss it with questions and comments along the following lines.

If you have a teenager, did this video make you feel a little better? Why or why not?

If you don't have a teenager yet, did this video scare you? Why or why not?

Do you think it's that hard to find a compliant teenager? On what do you base your answer?

Do you think helping your teen understand his or her physical changes would have an impact on your teen's behavior? Why or why not?

What are some specific opportunities in which you might do that?

Do you recognize any evidences of insecurity in your teen or a teen you know? How might you encourage him or her to see beyond the exterior?

If you have a teenager, do you feel you're on his or her "team"? Do you think he or she feels you are? If parents are reluctant to answer, just have them think about the issue.

STEP 4

BY THE BOOK

(5-10 minutes)

Have the group turn to the "WordWorks" Bible study section in the participant's guide. Let volunteers answer the questions found there.

1. LUKE 2:41-51

Would you say Jesus was being strong-willed here? How does His behavior compare to that of adolescents you've known? Opinions might vary. As needed, remind the group that having a strong will is not wrong. That may help some group members to acknowledge that Jesus appears here to have a strong will. Most probably will agree that His independence here is reminiscent of many adolescents.

Is it possible for a young person to be strong-willed and not defiant? How do you know? (Yes. A young person can be strong-willed, yet obedient and respectful.)

Is it any comfort to you that even Jesus and His earthly parents didn't see eye to eye all the time? Why or why not? (Most parents will likely be encouraged to see that even Mary and Joseph didn't always understand their adolescent.)

2. 1 SAMUEL 17:32-40, 50

Would you say that young David was strong-willed? Why or why not? (If he wasn't strong-willed, he was certainly difficult to persuade. David seemed to have an answer for every option Saul offered, and wasn't willing to concede much ground.)

What positive attributes of a strong-willed adolescent are displayed in this story? (Some possibilities: the ability to stand up for oneself; communicating forcefully with adults; self-confidence.)

David went on to be king of Israel. If you have (or someday will have) a strong-willed teenager, what will be your hope for him or her? Responses will vary. Encourage parents to see a teenager's strong will as a potential asset, not just a challenge.

STEP 5

WORK IT OUT

(10 minutes)

Turn with your group to the "Your Way" section in the participant's guide. Give people at least five minutes to work through the activities individually. If time is short, form two teams; Team 1 should discuss Item 1 and Team 2 should address Items 2 & 3.

If time allows, let volunteers share what they've learned or planned.

Close the session with prayer, asking for specific requests about challenging issues any parents are facing with their kids. Encourage people to read the participant's guide's "Tech Support" tips from Dr. Dobson this week as they work at disciplining their teens and teens-to-be.

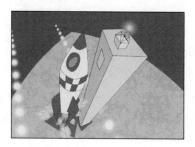

THE STRONG-WILLED ADOLESCENT, PART 2

SESSION AIM   To help group members go deeper into the unique challenge of maintaining a relationship with strong-willed adolescents.

SCRIPTURES FOR STUDY   Luke 2:41-51; Psalm 78:5-7

SETTING THE STAGE   • Before the session, group members should read and complete these sections in chapter 11 of their participant's guides: "Home Base," "Your Story," and "WordWorks."
• Cue up the video to segment 11, "The Strong-Willed Adolescent, Part 2."
• You'll also need pens or pencils, plus supplies for any of the "Willpower Olympics" activities you choose (see step 1).

STARTING OUT   "The more rebellious and frustrating your kid is, the more likely you are to give too much, tolerate too much, advise too much, and rescue too much. These blunders come down to a common thread—one that results from hanging on too tightly when you should be letting go. In so doing, you run the risk of making emotional cripples out of your recently minted adults.

"I have been suggesting that parents be willing to take whatever corrective action is required during the adolescent years, but to do it without nagging, moaning, groaning, and growling. Let love be your guide! Even though it often doesn't seem like it, your teen desperately wants to be loved and to feel connected to you. Anger does not motivate teenagers. That is why the parent or teacher who can find the delicate balance between love and firm discipline is the one who ends up winning the heart of teenagers. The adult who screams and threatens but does not love is only going to fuel teenage rebellion."

—Dr. James Dobson in *The New Strong-Willed Child*
(Tyndale House)

Step 1

All in This Together

(5-10 minutes)

Start the session by staging a rematch of the "Willpower Olympics." Whoever was the strongest-willed person last week, engage one or more challengers to take him or her on for the following challenge:

- Ask a volunteer to read the quote from Dr. Dobson in today's session as slowly and calmly as possible *in monotone* while the strongest-willed person heckles them, tickles them, or otherwise tries to break their concentration. After that, switch roles and have the heckler be the reader. Repeat with other challengers if time allows.

After the rematch, make the transition to this session's topic:

So, do we have a new strongest-willed person in our group?

How do you think this is applicable to raising teenagers? Allow people to respond with their opinions.

Understanding how to maintain a relationship with your teen when they insist on challenging your authority is what we're going to be discussing today.

Step 2

You Are Here

(5-10 minutes)

Direct your group to the "Your Story" section in their participant's guides. Have them discuss their answers with questions like the following:

Who recalls their teen's introduction to teenhood? Have a volunteer share his or her story. If there are no parents of teens in your group, ask instead, **What sort of things have you heard from other parents about the time they were confronted with the reality that they had a teenager in the house?**

Next, take a few responses to item 3. Again, if there are no parents of teens present or willing to share, ask for volunteers' answers to Item 4.

Wrap up this section by asking for a show of hands on the following question: **How many of you are learning right now about strong-willed teens from your own or someone else's?** As time allows, encourage volunteers to share what specifically they're learning.

STEP 3

SCREEN TIME

(15-30 minutes)

Play video segment 11, entitled, "The Strong-Willed Adolescent, Part 2." Make pencils or pens available for taking notes in the "Screen Time" section of the participant's guide.

After watching the video segment together, discuss it with questions and comments along the following lines.

By a show of hands, how many parents are going through a period of silence with their teen right now? How many anticipate one? Was anyone inspired to make better efforts at breaking through? Ask for volunteers to share responses as they feel led.

What are some of the tools for controlling the balance of freedom and limits? (Keys to the car, the family purse, use of telephone, stereo, TV, videos.)

Which of those would be hardest to your child? Why?

In the example of Danny, what do you think might have helped him? (Possible answers might be a parent or respected adult setting aside time to talk with the boy, affirming love for him, acknowledging his turmoil, etc.)

Dr. Dobson has said that the key to adolescent discipline, if one exists, involves the manipulation of circumstances. How might that look in your home? Encourage people to apply the principle to their own styles and situations. Examples might include such penalties as losing privileges and freedoms, and such rewards as increased independence.

If you were in Dr. Dobson's place, what advice would you add on disciplining strong-willed teenagers? (A few possibilities: Be consistent with consequences for disobedience; make sure disciplinary measures and boundaries are age-appropriate; listen to your teenager; give perspective to teen problems without making light of them; extend limits without abandoning them.)

STEP 4

BY THE BOOK

(5-10 minutes)

Have the group turn to the "WordWorks" Bible study section in the participant's guide. Let volunteers answer the questions found there.

1. LUKE 2:41-51

According to your answers about this passage last week, how would you say Jesus demonstrates the difference between strong will and defiance? Opinions might vary. As necessary, remind the group that independence is different than defiance, but let opinions be voiced freely.

How do you think Jesus knew so well where He belonged at such a young age? Do you see evidence in your child of this kind of security, or could it be improved? A strong-willed person can be trained to know where he or she belongs relative to God's will. Whether or not a teen accepts it is up to the individual.

No doubt, like all adolescents, Jesus learned from His parents, even while teaching them good parenting. What are some lessons you've received from your son or daughter? Have parents share as time allows. You might want to give extra time for sharing of responses here, if you're able.

2. PSALM 78:5-7

When you think of how your child might influence future generations, how does it make you feel? Which aspects of your current relationship do you think will be most beneficial to your grandchildren? Why? Have volunteers share their answers as they choose.

What attributes do you hope your child will carry on to your grandchildren? Some possibilities: the ability to stand up for oneself; communicating forcefully with adults; self-confidence, etc.

What does this passage indicate as the key to ensuring children know God's works and respect His commands? (Forefathers teaching their children.) **Why is respect for God's law so important?** Responses will vary. Encourage freedom among responses and opinions given.

STEP 5

WORK IT OUT

(10 minutes)

Turn with your group to the "Your Way" section in the participant's guide. Give people at least five minutes to work through the activities individually. If time is short, form two teams; Team 1 should work through Item 1 and Team 2 should address Item 2.

If time allows, let volunteers share what they've learned or planned.

Before closing the session, you may want to read the following recap on disciplining teens, taken from Dr. Dobson's *The New Strong-Willed Child* (Tyndale House):

"In summary, I have been suggesting that parents be willing to take whatever corrective action is required, but to avoid nagging, moaning, groaning, and growling when possible. Anger does not motivate teenagers! How foolish it is, for example, for the vice principal of Kamikaze High School to stand screaming in the parking lot as students roar past in their cars. He can solve the speeding problem once and for all by placing a bump in the road which will tear the wheels off their love-buggies if they ignore its sinister presence. In Russia, by the way, students who are convicted of taking drugs are placed at the end of a waiting list to obtain cars. This policy has had a remarkable impact on the unpopularity of narcotics there, I'm told. These two illustrations contain the key to adolescent discipline, if in fact one exists. It involves the manipulation of circumstances, whatever they may be, to influence the behavior of youngsters, combined with an appeal to love and reason and cooperation and compromise."

Close the session by asking for parenting-related prayer requests and praying about them. Encourage people to read the participant's guide's "Tech Support" tips from Dr. Dobson this week as they work at understanding their teens and teens-to-be.

SESSION 12

THE ULTIMATE PRIORITY

SESSION AIM
To help group members understand the importance of cultivating their children's relationship with God, and to help them plan ways to do so.

SCRIPTURES FOR STUDY
Deuteronomy 6:6-9; Proverbs 3:1-6

SETTING THE STAGE
- Before the session, group members should read and complete these sections in chapter 12 of their participant's guides: "Home Base," "Your Story," and "WordWorks."
- Cue up the video to segment 12, "The Ultimate Priority."
- You'll also need pencils or pens.

STARTING OUT
The best approach is found in the instruction given to the children of Israel by Moses more than four thousand years ago (Deuteronomy 6:7-9). This commandment provides the key to effective spiritual training at home. It isn't enough to pray with your children each night, although family devotions are important. We must live the principles of faith throughout the day. References to the Lord and our

beliefs should permeate our conversation and our interactions with our kids. Our love for Jesus should be understood to be the first priority in our lives. We must miss no opportunities to teach the components of our theology and the passion that is behind it. I believe this teaching task is the most important assignment God has given to us as parents.

— Dr. James Dobson in *The Complete Marriage and Family Home Reference Guide* (Tyndale House)

STEP 1

ALL IN THIS TOGETHER

(5-10 minutes)

Ask your group: **What happens if your children don't get enough of the following?**
- Food
- Water
- Physical exercise
- Vocational training
- Clothing
- Spiritual guidance

Then ask: **If that were a priority list, where would you put "spiritual guidance"? Why?**

Now here's a question to think about, not answer aloud: Are you satisfied with the spiritual training your children are getting?

After giving people a few moments to consider that, explain: **In today's video, Dr. James Dobson talks about the ultimate priority of parenting.**

STEP 2

YOU ARE HERE

(5-10 minutes)

Ask group members to turn to the "Your Story" section in the Participant's Guide. Invite responses to question 1 as they feel comfortable.

Can anyone share some ways you've given spiritual guidance to your children?

Three types of spiritual training are intentional training times, spontaneous "teachable moments," and leading by example. Is there an ideal balance between these three types? What should guide a parent's decision in choosing among the different types?

Wrap up this part of the chapter with a comment like the following:

Most busy parents agree that making spiritual guidance a priority can be difficult. Yet no matter how it's applied, spiritual training is vital in the life of every child. Let's hear what Dr. Dobson has to say about this ultimate priority of parenting.

STEP 3
SCREEN TIME

(15-30 minutes)

Pass out pencils or pens. Watch video segment 12, "The Ultimate Priority." Encourage participants to take notes in the "Screen Time" section of the Participant's Guide.

After watching the video segment together, discuss it with questions and comments along the following lines.

Did this video leave you feeling guilty, inspired, or something else? Why?

Would you agree that leading by example is the best way for Christian parents to teach children about spiritual matters? Why?

Read the following quote from Dr. Dobson's book *Bringing Up Boys*: "I believe the greatest sense of fulfillment as you prepare to close the final chapter [of life] will be in knowing that you lived by a consistent standard of holiness before God and that you invested yourself unselfishly in the lives of your family members and friends. . . . Why not determine to live according to that value system now, while you still have the opportunity to influence the impressionable kids who look up to you? This may be the most important question you as a mother or father will ever have to face!"

Ask: **How have you faced this question so far? Do you feel the need for change in this area? Why or why not?**

STEP 4
BY THE BOOK

(5-10 minutes)

Have the group turn to the "WordWorks" section of the Participant's Guide. Read, or have a volunteer read, Deuteronomy 6:6-9. Then ask questions like the following.

According to verse 6, who needs to learn God's commands? (All of us. God's truths are to be on our own hearts—preferably before we try to pass them on.)

What advice does this passage give on how to teach God's commands to children? (Talk about them during everyday activities;

put them in prominent places around the house, even on yourself.)

What would be the best places in your home to put Bible verses if you wanted your children to see them often?

Ask a volunteer to read Proverbs 3:1-6. Then ask questions like these:

According to Solomon, what will following his instruction give his son? (Longer life, prosperity, favor and a good reputation with God and people.)

After listing these benefits, what is the first instruction Solomon gives? ("Trust in the Lord.")

Do your children understand the importance and benefits of trusting in the Lord? How do you know? If group members would prefer not to share this personal information, just let them think about it.

STEP 5

WORK IT OUT

(10 minutes)

Have people turn to the "Your Way" section of the Participant's Guide and spend a few minutes gauging where their children are spiritually. Allow group members to work on this individually. Let volunteers share results. If group members are reluctant to do so, due to the personal nature of the information, don't press. Simply encourage people to use their answers as indicators of areas they need to work on.

If time allows, form pairs or teams who pray for each other and for their kids—especially for progress in their children's relationship with God. If your church offers special programs for spiritual development, encourage parents to consider them.

Call attention to the "Tech Support" section of the Participant's Guide and encourage the group to keep in touch with each other as they work to implement these final, most important principles.

Thank everyone for their participation and close the session with a prayer that each child represented by these parents will be blessed.

THAT'S A WRAP

REVIEWING AND RESPONDING

This session is built to help your group review what you've learned, and to catch up on principles you didn't have time to cover. It's less structured than other sessions in this course, giving you freedom to address concepts you feel are most needed by your group.

You'll need refreshments, pens or pencils, and paper. If possible, remind people to bring their participant's guides; you'll be asking group members to complete some exercises they didn't have time to finish before.

STEP 1

SUCESSES & STRUGGLES

(10 minutes)

Give group members a chance to help themselves to whatever refreshments you've brought. Encourage them to eat while you convene a casual, whole-group discussion.

Ask questions like these:

When it comes to applying what we've discussed in this course, do you have any "success stories" to share?

If possible, bring one or two examples of your own. If people are reluctant to respond because their successes don't seem impressive, remind them that even the tiniest "victories" are progress. If participants can't recall all the topics that were addressed, help them with questions like the following.

Have you come up with any new boundaries at home? How has your child reacted?

Have you stood up to your child's willful defiance? What happened?

Have you tried taking action *before* getting angry? What happened?

How have you been more loving in your discipline?

Are you spanking more or less than you did before the course started? Why?

Have you used any new rewards or penalties? What's been the result?

What progress are you making in extinguishing one of your child's bad habits?

How is your discipline more age-appropriate than it used to be?

What have you been doing to balance shaping your child's will with protecting his or her spirit?

Are you yelling at your child less than you used to? Why or why not?

Do you see your child developing any self-discipline, or needing less direction from you?

Chances are that some parents will feel less than successful in some or all of these areas. Assure them that most parenting principles take much longer to live out than they do to learn. For those with no "success stories," ask:

Even if you don't see visible results, have any of your attitudes changed for the better during this course?

In trying to apply the concepts of this course, have you made any mistakes from which the rest of us might learn?

What's the biggest challenge you've faced as you've tried to apply a principle from this course?

STEP 2

CLEARING THE AIR

(10 minutes)

Next, allow group members to openly share their opinions and feelings about the course itself. Encourage them to be honest, and assure them that there are no "wrong" answers to the questions you're about to ask.

What did you like about his course? Why?

What did you disagree with during this course, if anything?

If some take issue with opinions expressed during the course, don't worry. You don't have to defend positions that were taken. Simply ask dissenters to explain their reasoning and thank them for expressing themselves.

Did you feel that any important points were missed? If so, what? Is there anything we discussed that you wish could be clarified?

As needed, let others in the group offer explanations if some are confused about certain principles. If no one has a good answer, don't panic. Refer people to Dr. Dobson's books, especially *The Complete Marriage and Family Home Reference Guide* (Tyndale House), for help. If you can, offer to help questioners find answers after your meeting.

Step 3

Unfinished Business

(15-25 minutes)

Have group members glance through the "Your Story" sections of the Participant's Guide for exercises they haven't had time to complete. Say something like this:

As James 2:17 reminds us, "Faith by itself, if it is not accompanied by action, is dead." Let's take some time to make sure the words we heard and spoke in this course lead to action. Which action steps in the "Your Story" sections did you have to leave unfinished? Find a partner and work together on completing those action steps.

Allow plenty of time for partners to do this. In the unlikely event that some group members completed all the "Your Story" sections already, have them spend this time writing evaluations of how well they followed through on their action steps.

After fifteen minutes or so, let volunteers share the results of their work with the rest of the group. Affirm as many ideas as you can, and encourage people to follow through this week.

Step 4

Keeping in Touch

(10-15 minutes)

Urge group members to stay in touch with and support each other as they continue the awesome job of parenting. To help them do that, try one or more of the following:

- Pass around a sign-up sheet on which people can write their names, addresses, phone numbers, and/or e-mail addresses. Make it clear that this is voluntary. Photocopy the list after the meeting and see that everyone on the list gets a copy.

- Plan a reunion for three months from now. Group members will be able to get back together, swap "war stories," and pray for each other and their kids.
- Encourage parents to set up informal get-togethers (not necessarily as the whole group) for picnics or play dates.
- Suggest that group members ask others to be their prayer-and-accountability partners. This might involve talking once a week, in person or on the phone, about how things are going.

To close, form small groups. Encourage people to share prayer requests about their parenting challenges, and to pray specifically for each other. Wrap up the session with a prayer of your own, asking God to bless each group member with wisdom and to help each person enjoy his or her children in the days and years to come.

enjoy the journey™

Does parenting sometimes seem like an overwhelming task? Your role as a parent is difficult but very important to you and your children, and Focus on the Family® wants to encourage you! The complimentary Focus on Your Child® membership program has age-specific materials that provide timely encouragement, advice and information for today's busy parents. With newsletters or audio journals delivered straight to your doorstep once a month and a Web site packed with over 900 articles, Focus on Your Child can help you enjoy the journey!

Here's what the membership includes:

Parenting Newsletters: Four age-specific and concise editions for parents with no spare time.

Audio Journals: Timely information for parents and fun activities for children, based on their ages.

Online Resources: Age-customized articles, e-mail news, recommended resources and topic-organized forum through which parents can share with one another.

To sign up, go to www.focusonyourchild.com or call (800) A-FAMILY.

YF05XPRD